Armed & Victorious

A 30-Day Devotional for Women in Spiritual Warfare

Lesa Henderson

Dedication

To My heavenly father, who chose me, kept me and enabled me by His strength and His son and His spirit. You are my redeemer and rock. My hiding place. May I always abide deeply in you.

To every woman who has ever felt weary in the battle. May you discover that you are never fighting alone.

May you learn to stand clothed in Christ, rooted in His truth, and confident in His victory.

And may you always remember who you are in Him—chosen, redeemed, loved, and armed for every battle.

To my husband, Ken and Children, Brandon, Tiffany & Destiny who have walked through intense warfare with me. *We are still standing strong.* The four of you make me so proud; you are a testimony of God's faithfulness, mercy and goodness. I love you more than breath. Jesus is King.

Introduction

Dear Sister in Christ,

For thirty years, starting in 1995, I have had the privilege of ministering to women like you. I've shared conversations over coffee and in church classrooms, listened to stories of heartbreak and exhaustion, and walked with women through unexpected seasons. I've seen marriages under pressure, mothers worn out from struggles with their children, and faithful women hurt by division in their churches or by the challenges in our nation. Through it all, one truth remains: **you are not alone. God is with you, and He has already given you what you need for victory.**

Whether you are single or married, raising children or praying for loved ones, serving in ministry or just trying to get through the day, the enemy's strategy is always the same: to make you feel alone, overwhelmed, and powerless. But here's the good news: **Jesus has already won.** In Him, we don't fight *for* victory; we fight *from* victory.

This truth is the foundation of this devotional.

I want to be clear from the start. I believe in spiritual warfare and in the authority of Jesus' name. I believe in binding and loosing, rebuking the enemy, and standing against his attacks. I believe in closing doors that have given the enemy access.

I believe in deliverance and the power and authority of the name of Jesus. I've practiced and lived this many times over the years. But *Armed & Victorious* isn't a manual to teach you to fight harder, pray louder, or always look for what you might have missed.

I wrote this devotional because I've seen what happens when spiritual warfare is based on technique without closeness to God, formulas without knowing who we are, or effort without truly abiding in Him. Too often, women end up living in fear—worried they didn't pray the right way, that something slipped through, or that they failed spiritually when things didn't get better. That kind of warfare doesn't bring freedom; it only leads to exhaustion.

This devotional is about drawing closer to God, not working harder. It's about learning to stand firm *in Christ*, not always trying to stay ahead of the enemy. It's about resting in who you are and who you belong to, because real authority comes from intimacy with God, not from worry.

That's why I wrote *Armed & Victorious:* to walk with you for 30 days as you learn to put on the full armor of God and stand strong in the real battles you face each day, rooted in your relationship with Jesus.

Here's what you'll find in these pages:

Each day starts with a key Scripture from the New Living Translation, followed by a short devotional from my heart to yours. You'll read relatable stories, honest encouragement, and biblical truth that connects to real life. There's a practical **Application** to help you live out God's truth, a heartfelt **Prayer** to bring your needs to the Lord, and a **Journal Prompt** to help you reflect and grow.

Most importantly, each day ends with **Take Up Your Sword**—four bold, Scripture-based declarations for you to say out loud. This is your chance to use the Sword of the Spirit, the Word of God, as described in Ephesians 6:17. These declarations aren't about controlling what happens, but about bringing our hearts, minds, and faith in line with what God has already said. When we speak His truth, our faith grows stronger, lies lose their power, and we remember the authority we have in Christ. If you use the companion audio prayers, I'll guide you through each prayer and declaration so we can speak God's truth together.

During these 30 days, we'll start by recognizing the reality of the battle and finding our strength in the Lord. Next, we'll look closely at each piece of God's armor, beginning with Ephesians 6 and then discovering how the armor points us to Christ. We'll apply what it means to be clothed in Him to everyday struggles like anxiety, relationships, identity, purpose, and calling. We'll end with themes of perseverance, community, resilience, and encouragement to keep walking boldly in Christ.

My prayer is that when you finish this book, you will feel **armed, confident, and victorious**—not because life gets easier, but because you know who you are in Christ, how to stand firm when the enemy attacks, and how to live in the freedom and authority Jesus has given you. You are not defined by your struggles or feelings. You are not a victim; you are a warrior, learning to stand strong in Him. And greater is He who is in you than he who is in the world.

Let's suit up together.

With love and faith
Lesa Henderson

Contents

SECTION I:

AWAKENED AND POSITIONED

Before we talk about armor, strategy, or standing firm, pause with me.
Close your eyes and remember a moment when you felt deep stillness—perhaps during worship, in prayer, or alone at dawn before the world stirred awake. There is often a quiet sense of anticipation before something significant unfolds.

Feel that moment right before the trumpet sounds—a hush settling over the camp, like dawn air holding its breath.

We begin here.

Spiritual warfare does not start with action; it begins with clarity.

> *Spiritual warfare simply means recognizing that we face real opposition, not just from our own weaknesses but from spiritual forces that want to distract and discourage us.*

Many believers sense resistance, pressure, or opposition long before they can name what is happening. Others feel the weight of battle without understanding why it feels so personal or relentless.

This section is about awakening to the reality of the battle **without fear** and positioning yourself on the unshakable foundation of Christ.

You are not being called to become hyper-aware of the enemy.

You are being called to become anchored in the Lord.

Scripture tells us to *"be strong in the Lord and in His mighty power"* before we are ever told to stand. Strength flows from knowing where you stand—and who you stand in.

In these opening days, we will name the battle honestly while rooting you firmly in Christ as your solid rock.

This is not about striving or bracing for impact.

It is about discovering that you are already held, already equipped, and already positioned in Him.

From this place—secure, grounded, and awake—we move forward.

Before reading on, pause and open your heart to receive His strength as a gift.

You might pray:

"Lord, I open my hands to Your power. Root me deeper than my fears and fill me with Your strength as I stand in You."

Day 1: Awakening to the Battle

Key Scripture

"For we are not fighting against flesh-and-blood enemies,
but against evil rulers and authorities of the unseen world,
against mighty powers in this dark world,
and against evil spirits in the heavenly places."
Ephesians 6:12 (NLT)

Reflection

Sister, have you ever walked through a day feeling strangely heavy, but you can't quite explain why? Maybe the air at the breakfast table turns thick after one sharp comment, and the silence that follows feels louder than any argument. Or a small disagreement with your husband clings to you all day like a weight you can't shake. Then, when the house finally quiets down at night, anxiety slips in right as you're trying to rest.

It all feels so human, so ordinary, so painfully *every day*, but Scripture reminds us that something more is happening. There is a real spiritual battle taking place for your heart, your relationships, and every area of your life.

The war does not define you—Jesus does.

Closing Spiritual Seal

You are not defined by the struggle in front of you.

Before any attack ever formed against you, your Father already named you His beloved daughter.

Application

Find five quiet minutes today—step outside, sit in your car, or close the door to your bedroom if you need to.

Ask the Holy Spirit to highlight one area where the pressure feels especially strong right now: a strained relationship, a financial weight, an old wound that keeps resurfacing, or a fear about what lies ahead.

Simply admit it to Him and ask, "Lord, show me what is really happening here. Help me see this through Your eyes."

Prayer

Father, I invite You into the places where I feel tired and confused.

Open my eyes to the spiritual battle behind the surface of my circumstances. When I feel overwhelmed, remind me that I am not alone—You are near, Your Spirit lives in me, and Your strength is enough for this moment.

In Jesus' name, amen.

Take Up Your Sword

Speak these truths aloud with faith

- I am awake to the spiritual battle around me. *(Romans 13:11)*

- My struggle is not against people, but against defeated powers. *(Ephesians 6:12; Colossians 2:15)*

Journal Prompt

- "Could this be more than just 'bad luck' or 'mood'?"

- "What specific promise or verse... pushes back against the lie"

Day 2: Standing Strong in the Lord

Key Scripture

"Be strong in the Lord and in his mighty power.
Put on all of God's armor so that you will be
able to stand firm against all strategies of the devil."
Ephesians 6:10–11 (NLT)

Reflection

Sister, you don't have to be strong by yourself, because you're not alone. Paul begins the armor passage with a simple but powerful command: "Be strong in the Lord." Our strength was never meant to come from us.

There is a real enemy who looks for moments when you feel exhausted, alone, or discouraged to take advantage (1 Peter 5:8). Dependence on God's power is our shield and strength. Standing strong isn't about trying harder; it's about trusting more in God's strength.

As women, we often carry heavy burdens without saying much. We keep going, even when we feel empty. But our victory doesn't come from pushing ourselves harder; it comes from letting go and trusting God. Fighting spiritual battles on our own is like trying to power a city with a small battery rather than an endless power source. When we depend on the Lord, His strength meets us right where ours ends.

I remember a time when I was deeply worried about my children and my marriage. Praying felt hard, answers seemed far away, and I was almost out of strength. One day, after crying out to God with my face pressed into the carpet, tears made a puddle on the floor. In that quiet, I felt Him say, *"I am here. You are not alone."* My situation didn't change right away, but I did. When I let go of what I was carrying, His peace found me, and His strength helped me through what I couldn't handle alone.

Real strength is knowing where to turn when you do feel weak.

Standing strong in the Lord doesn't mean you never feel weak. In fact, even Paul, who wrote this very letter, admitted to carrying a "thorn in his flesh"—a weakness he pleaded with God to take away. Instead, God's answer to him was, "My grace is sufficient for you, for my power is made perfect in weakness." When you feel frail, you are in good company and exactly where God's grace can shine brightest.

Closing Spiritual Seal

Let the whisper of Jesus fill your heart, *"Beloved, the cross has decided the outcome long before this battle started. I have already won this victory for you. You are seated with Me, not struggling to hold your place."*

Stand firm today in the place He has already secured for you.

Application

Take five quiet minutes today. Ask the Holy Spirit to show you one burden you have been carrying by yourself. Write it down. Then, to seal your surrender, tear up or safely burn the paper, symbolically giving that burden to the Lord. Remember, you were never meant to carry it alone.

Speak this declaration aloud three times:

"I am strong in the Lord and in His mighty power—not in my own."

Prayer

Lord, I admit that I've been trying to fight in my own strength, and I'm tired. Today, I choose to be strong in You alone. Fill me with Your mighty power and help me stand firm against every scheme of the enemy. I surrender my battles, my fears, and my weaknesses to You. Thank You for being my strength and my shield. In Jesus' name, Amen.

Take Up Your Sword

(Speak these truths aloud throughout the day)

- I am strong in the Lord's mighty power. (Ephesians 6:10)

- I put on God's full armor and stand firm. (Ephesians 6:11)

- The Lord is my strength and shield; I will not be shaken. (Psalm 28:7; Psalm 62:6)

- No weapon formed against me will prosper. (Isaiah 54:17)

Journal Prompt

What burden have you been trying to carry in your own strength?

How might trusting God's strength instead of your own change the way you face that situation today?

SECTION II:

Dressed for Battle

Key Scripture

"Put on all of God's armor so that you will be able to stand firm against all strategies of the devil."
Ephesians 6:11 (NLT)

Introduction

Some time ago, I found myself exhausted by a string of discouragements — unexpected setbacks, relationships growing distant, and an overwhelming sense of spiritual fatigue that seemed to settle in overnight. In the middle of a restless night, I realized how easily I had slipped into trying to fight these battles in my own strength, unaware of just how unguarded I was. That moment jolted me awake to the reality of the battle surrounding us all. Awakening to the battle is only the beginning. Once we understand where we stand, Scripture invites us to be intentionally clothed for what lies ahead.

Spiritual warfare is not first about what you do—it's about what you wear.

This section is not a call to fight harder or watch for what you might have missed. Over the next 14 days, we turn our attention to the armor of God—not as a list of spiritual tasks, but as a divine provision given out of God's love and care for His people. Too often, we can approach passages like these with a mental checklist, quickly ticking off 'truth,' 'righteousness,' or 'faith' as if we are simply completing spiritual chores before moving on. The armor is not about becoming aggressive or hyper-focused on the enemy. It is about being properly covered so that we can remain steady, discerning, and unshaken in the midst of real opposition.

Here, we will slow down and look carefully at what God has provided for our protection and endurance. When Paul described the armor of God to the first believers in Ephesus, Roman soldiers were part of daily life. The weight of bronze and leather, the gleam of a breastplate in the sun, the sound of sandals on ancient stone streets—these were vivid, tangible reminders of strength and readiness. In the same way, we will learn how the armor functions, why each piece matters, and how God intends it to be worn—not occasionally, but daily.

This section unfolds in two movements. In ***Movement One: Understanding the Armor of God,*** we will gain an understanding of the armor as Scripture presents it. Yet what if the armor is less about equipment and more about identity? What if these pieces are not merely spiritual gear, but a reflection of something deeper? With that question in mind, we will go deeper in ***Movement Two: Clothed in Christ***—exploring how the armor is not just something we put on, but a vivid picture of who Christ is and who we are in Him.

This is not about learning what to wear for battle.

Picture this: it's a hectic Monday morning. Maybe you're packing lunches, helping with lost homework, chasing after little ones, and trying to grab a quick cup of coffee before the day sweeps you away. Or perhaps your mornings are quieter—maybe you're single or retired, and the house is still, but the challenges you face are no less real. Loneliness, changing seasons, or navigating new routines can require just as much strength. In that moment, putting on God's armor might sound abstract—but what if, as you slip on your shoes, you pause and pray, "Lord, fit me with readiness today. Guard my heart; cover my mind with Your truth." Just as you wouldn't leave the house without dressing, you can choose to clothe yourself with God's armor before facing the day. Making this a part of your everyday routine doesn't take extra time; it's simply an intentional invitation for His strength to cover you right where life is busiest—or quietest.

It is about learning how to live clothed in Christ.

Inviting His presence, protection, and perspective into the ordinary rhythms of our hours.

MOVEMENT I:

Understanding the Armor of God

Before we can live clothed in Christ, we need to understand what Scripture tells us about the armor of God.

Many women are familiar with the language of spiritual armor yet have never been given space to slow down and understand it—not as a checklist, but as a provision rooted in God's care. For some, the concept of spiritual battle is linked with personal struggles or everyday stress. For others, the word battle carries very real weight, shaped by cultural realities, family history, or experiences that may not fit traditional or militaristic images. Still others have encountered the armor only in moments of crisis, reaching for it reactively rather than resting in it daily.

As we begin, I invite you to name your own battles—whatever they may look like. Your journey, shaped by your background, responsibilities, or the world you live in, will inform how these words speak to your heart. The armor described in Ephesians was based on first-century Roman military imagery, which can feel distant from our modern context. We approach it not to glorify conflict, but to recognize how God speaks into our real lives with empathy and understanding. This movement is designed to bring clarity, not pressure.

In the days ahead, we will walk carefully through each piece of the armor described in Ephesians 6. We will look at what it is, why it matters, and how God intends it to function in your everyday life. This is not about mastering technique or striving to "get it right," but about recognizing what God has already supplied for your protection and endurance.

Think of this movement as learning the language of the armor—so that when we go deeper, you are standing on understanding, not assumption. As you read, allow the Holy Spirit to highlight where you may have misunderstood, rushed past, or carried unnecessary weight. Perhaps you have believed, "I have to earn God's protection," or thought, "God's armor is only for those who are always strong." Let the truth meet you here: God's armor is a gift, not a reward, and His provision comes from His love, not our effort. Take a moment to notice if any false narratives have shaped your view of spiritual armor. Ask God to help you set those down and receive what He freely gives. There is no rush here. God is patient, and His provision is complete.

You are not being trained to fight harder. You are being called into God's restful strength—a place where His peace, or shalom, brings wholeness and flourishing even during life's challenges.

You are being invited to see more clearly.

From this place of understanding, we will move into something deeper, learning what it means not just to wear the armor, but to be clothed in Christ Himself. Imagine the gentle weight of His presence settling around you like a soft, radiant cloak, wrapping you in warmth and light. This is an invitation to an intimacy that can be felt as surely as fabric on your skin—Christ's nearness woven around your heart, offering protection and peace that you can sense in every moment.

It is about learning how to live clothed in Christ.

So, step forward today in the radiance of the One who already covers you.

Day 3: Dressed for Battle

"Put on all of God's armor so that you will be able to stand firm against all strategies of the devil."
Ephesians 6:11 (NLT)

Reflection

Sister, imagine a soldier stepping onto the battlefield without protective gear. It would be unthinkable and dangerous.

But what about us? Picture yourself in the chaos of a typical morning: rushing to find your car keys, coffee tipping as you grab your bag, your mind tumbling through endless to-do lists before you even reach the door. The world already feels full of little battles—distractions, frustrations, worries—before the day has really begun. Yet many of us rush into these moments without intentionally putting on the spiritual armor God has already provided.

The battles we face aren't just emotional, relational, or circumstantial.

Scripture makes it clear: there is an unseen spiritual war, and God has not left us unprotected. The enemy often attacks with subtle, persistent lies—like "You're on your own," or "You're overlooked" or "God is disappointed in you," or "Things will never change." These strategies are designed to erode our trust in God's goodness and keep us isolated. Paul's instruction is simple and powerful: put *on all of God's armor.* Not some of it. Not only the pieces we remember or prefer. Every piece matters.

Here is what our Commander has given us:

- **The Belt of Truth** – Anchors us in God's Word and holds everything together.

- **The Breastplate of Righteousness** – Guards our hearts with

Christ's righteousness, protecting us from shame and accusation.

- **The Shoes of the Gospel of Peace** – Keep us steady and ready to walk in peace wherever God sends us.

- **The Shield of Faith** – Extinguishes every fiery arrow of fear, doubt, and temptation.

- **The Helmet of Salvation** – Protects our minds with the assurance of who we are in Christ.

- **The Sword of the Spirit** – The Word of God, our offensive weapon against lies and deception.

- **Prayer** – The posture that keeps us connected, alert, and dependent on God's power.

There was a season when anxiety seemed like a constant assault on my mind, thoughts coming fast and unrelenting. It wasn't until I began intentionally "dressing for battle" each morning—praying through each piece of armor—that peace returned. The circumstances did not disappear, but I was no longer unprotected. This daily habit became part of a broader spiritual rhythm alongside Scripture meditation and prayer.

"You were never meant to fight unarmed—God has already dressed you for victory."

Step into today fully equipped.

Closing Spiritual Seal

The armor is God's provision for daily victory. When you intentionally put it on, you choose to depend on His strength rather than your own

Move forward today grounded in truth, not reaction.

Application

Create a simple **Spiritual Armor Checklist**. Write down each piece of the armor (including prayer) on a note card or in your phone. Beginning tomorrow morning, take a few minutes to pray through the list, intentionally "putting on" each piece before you start your day.

Prayer

Father God, thank You for providing everything I need to stand firm. Today, I choose to put on the full armor You have given me—the Belt of Truth, the Breastplate of Righteousness, the Shoes of Peace, the Shield of Faith, the Helmet of Salvation, and I take up the Sword of the Spirit. Teach me to stay clothed in Your strength and covered by Your protection. I depend on You, not myself. In Jesus' name, Amen.

Take Up Your Sword

(Speak these truths aloud)

- I put on the full armor of God today—every piece, nothing missing. *(Ephesians 6:11,13)*

- I am dressed for battle and fully equipped by the Lord. *(2 Corinthians 10:4; Romans 13:12)*

- God's armor protects me and empowers me to stand firm. *(Ephesians 6:13; Isaiah 54:17)*

- I walk in Christ's victory, confident and secure. *(1 Corinthians 15:57; Romans 8:37)*

Journal Prompt:

Which piece of the armor do you most need to be intentional about right now? How might your days change if you consciously "put it on" each morning?

Day 4: Resist and Remain – Equipped for the Evil Day

"Therefore, put on every piece of God's armor so you will be able to resist the enemy in the time of evil. Then after the battle, you will still be standing firm."
Ephesians 6:13 (NLT)

Reflection

Sister, notice how Paul doubles down on this. Just two verses earlier, he said, "put on all of God's armor," and now it's "put on *every piece*." The Holy Spirit wants us to get it: only the full armor is enough.

This armor protects us from every enemy attack—imagine stepping onto a battlefield missing your shield or helmet. Even one unprotected spot leaves you wide open to a fiery dart. Maybe it's a critical thought you half-believe, envy taking root in a quiet moment, or fear whispering through the night.

Without full coverage, any of these can slip through and shake your confidence in God's love and purpose. Paul isn't suggesting; he's urging us not to leave *any* part exposed.

Partial armor creates gaps, and gaps make us vulnerable. Paul knew there would be "times of evil"—those seasons when attacks feel relentless, drag on forever, and hit right where it hurts most. Maybe you're living one now: a strained marriage, kids struggling, health that won't cooperate, church tension, money stretched thin, fear pressing from every side. These are the days he's talking about.

But hear the promise woven right in: When you put on every piece of God's armor, you'll *resist* the enemy—and when the dust settles, you'll still be standing strong. Picture the battlefield gone quiet, smoke clearing, your feet planted firm while the enemy retreats. God isn't just helping you survive; He's building you unshakeable in faith, even through the longest fights.

I've walked those piling-on seasons myself—one challenge bleeding into the next: money tight, family frayed, accusations trying to derail my calling. It felt endless, like just when I'd catch my breath, another wave hit. You know that weight, even if your battles look different. I wondered if I could keep standing. But God showed me resisting isn't passive waiting; it's a daily choice. Standing firm meant suiting up in His armor every morning, speaking His truth aloud, refusing the enemy's lies. Because I stayed covered, I didn't just endure that season—I emerged stronger, steadier in my faith.

God's armor isn't for easy days;
it's what you need most when everything feels hard.

He hasn't left you defenseless in the storm—He's given you everything to stand and keep standing.

Lean in and listen to His gentle whisper: *"I am your strength and shield, My daughter."*

Closing Spiritual Seal

Resist the enemy and he will flee from you, not because of who you are but because of whose you are.

Christ is in you and God's presence is a shield around you.

Application

Name the "evil day" or pressing battle you are facing right now.

Write it down. Now create your declaration as a personal battle plan: Write beside your struggle, *"Because I am putting on every piece of God's armor, I will resist the enemy and still be standing when this is over."* Date your declaration, making it a spiritual milestone. Revisit it each week and reaffirm your stand, recording how God is helping you endure and remain strong.

Prayer

Father, thank You that You see every battle I face and have not left me unarmed. Today, I choose to put on every piece of Your armor. Strengthen me to resist the enemy's attacks and give me grace to keep standing when the battle feels long. Let me come through this season firm in faith and anchored in You. In the victorious name of Jesus, Amen.

Take Up Your Sword

(Speak these truths aloud)

- I put on every piece of God's armor. *(Ephesians 6:11,13)*

- I resist the enemy by Christ's power in me. (James 4:7; 1 *John 4:4)*

- After the battle, I will still be standing firm. *(Ephesians 6:13-14)*

- The Lord equips me fully, and I will not fall. *(2 Corinthians 1:21; Jude 1:24)*

Journal Prompt

What "evil day" or intense season are you walking through right now?

How does knowing God has fully equipped you to resist and remain change the way you face it today?

Who might notice your renewed stance this week—at home, work, or church?

Anticipate the difference your faith could make in someone else's life as you stand firm and let your resilience become a quiet testimony to His strength.

Day 5: Stand Your Ground – The Posture of Victory

Key Scripture

"...Then after the battle, you will still be standing firm. Stand your ground..."
Ephesians 6:14 (NLT)

Reflection

Sister, before Paul talks about any piece of armor, he repeats one command over and over: stand. In just a few verses, he tells us to stand firm and stand our ground several times. This repetition is on purpose.

Imagine Jesus leaning close and saying, *"I am inviting you to stand. I have already won the victory for you, so do not be afraid. Stand firm in Me."* He wants us to learn something important about spiritual battles.

We do not fight for victory; we fight from victory.

Jesus already defeated the enemy at the cross, disarming him and winning completely (Colossians 2:15). Because of Christ, we do not have to strive to win; instead, we trust in what He has already done. The enemy wants you to retreat, doubt your worth, or believe you must earn your place. But Scripture says you stand because you are in Christ, seated with Him in heavenly places (Ephesians 2:6). This truth gives you confidence and peace, knowing God is always with you.

There have been times when I did not feel steady at all. Pressures from ministry, family struggles, and the enemy's accusations made me feel knocked down and unsure of where I belonged. But God kept reminding me of one simple instruction: stand. Not perform better. Not try harder. But plant my feet on what Jesus has already done and refuse to give up any ground.

Standing your ground is not about being stubborn or relying on your own strength; it is an act of faith. It means choosing to trust what Christ has already done, not just what you feel right now. When you stand, you are saying, "This is where God has placed me, and I will not be moved." You hold your ground in your marriage, your thoughts, your family, and your calling --because the One who lives in you is greater than anything that comes against you.

Standing firm shows up in ordinary moments too. Think about your daily commute: traffic gets worse, frustration rises, but you pause, breathe, and ask God for patience instead of snapping. Or when you scroll through social media and comparison tries to creep in, you choose to remember your worth in Christ instead of letting insecurity win. Even in budgeting, holding your ground might mean trusting God with your needs and resisting the urge to worry or overspend. These are simple ways steadfast faith shows up in the middle of regular life.

Today, before you put on any piece of armor, pause for a moment. Let this become your mini ritual: **Pause. Breathe. Stand.** As you pause, quiet your heart. As you breathe, remember who you are in Christ. Then, take your stand. You are not falling back or running away—you are standing firm in the victory your King has already won.

Closing Spiritual Seal

Because you are seated with Christ, you do not need to panic or try to prove yourself. You stand firm, rooted on the solid rock. Take a moment now to let your heart become quiet **and listen for God's gentle voice, reminding you of His nearness**, *"Beloved, be still now, and let My Presence settle over you like armor; I am your victory, and I am here."*

Let the assurance of being with Christ settle deep within you.

Application

Take a quiet moment today. Stand up, plant your feet firmly on the ground, and say out loud:

"In Jesus' name, I stand my ground. I will not be moved."

Come back to this posture whenever you feel pressure to give up or step back.

Prayer

Father, thank You that Jesus has already won the victory, and I fight from that place. You know the exact battle I face today, the struggles and pressures only You can truly see. Please forgive me for the times I have stepped back in fear or shame.

Today I take my stand, not in my own strength, but in Yours. I plant my feet on the truth of Your Word and what Jesus finished on the cross. Give me strength to stay firm, no matter what comes against me. In the mighty name of Jesus, Amen.

Take Up Your Sword

(Speak these truths aloud)

- *Jesus won, so I stand. (1 Corinthians 15:57; Colossians 2:15)*

- I refuse to step back. *(Ephesians 6:13; James 4:7)*

- I am seated with Christ. *(Ephesians 2:6; Colossians 1:13)*

- I stand firm on Christ, my rock. *(Ephesians 6:13-14; Matthew 7:24-25)*

Journal Prompt

Where do you feel pressure to step back or give up right now? What would it look like to stand firm in Christ's victory in that area today?

What victory story will you record tonight as you see God at work on your behalf?

Expect Him to move and let your journal become a testimony of His faithfulness.

Day 6: The Belt of Truth – Secured Identity

"Stand your ground, putting on the belt of truth..."
Ephesians 6:14a (NLT)

Reflection

Sister, let's start with the first piece of armor Paul talks about: the belt of truth. For a Roman soldier, the belt was crucial. It kept the tunic in place, held the sword, and made sure everything stayed secure so the soldier could move freely and fight well. Without the belt, the rest of the armor would not work properly.

The belt of truth works the same way in our spiritual lives. It keeps everything together. If we do not hold on to truth, we can fall into deception, confusion, and instability. The Bible calls the enemy "the father of lies" (John 8:44), and his main tactic is deception. He attacks your thoughts and your identity, whispering lies about God, about you, and about what is really happening.

As women, we often recognize these lies: comparing ourselves to others and losing our joy, feeling shame from past hurts, feeling pressure to be perfect as wives, mothers, or leaders, or hearing the quiet voice that says we are not enough. But the enemy's lies go broader than that. Some of us feel we need to achieve a certain level of career success, keep up with expectations around body image, or prove our worth through social status or financial security. We may be told that unless we meet cultural standards of beauty, ability, or accomplishment, we do not measure up. These pressures can come from our families, workplaces, communities, or what we see online. When we believe these lies, they grip our hearts and steal our freedom.

The Belt of Truth is God's answer. Truth does not depend on feelings, culture, or circumstances. It comes from God's unchanging Word and from Jesus Christ Himself. Jesus said, "I am the way, the truth, and the life" (John 14:6). When you choose to hold on to His truth—His Word, His promises, and His perspective—the lies lose their power. Truth gives you a secure identity. You are beloved (1 John 3:1), chosen (Ephesians 1:4), forgiven (Ephesians 1:7), and empowered (Ephesians 3:20) through Christ.

I remember one evening, after a particularly rough day, sitting alone in my car in the driveway with only the glow of the streetlights coming through the windows. The day had been heavy with small failures, and my thoughts sounded louder in the quiet. I heard the enemy reminding me of every way I had fallen short as a wife and mother, telling me my mistakes meant I could never fulfill my calling. Waves of guilt and inadequacy washed over me. In that quiet, it felt like the lies were winning. But right there, in the stillness of that nighttime moment, the Lord gently opened my eyes to whose voice I was listening to. He reminded me that I was hearing the father of lies, not my loving Father in heaven. That became the turning point. I paused, breathed in God's kindness, and chose to anchor my heart and mind in His truth instead of my feelings. My circumstances did not immediately change but how I viewed them and what I thought did.

Lean in and hear His whisper, *"Beloved, let My truth anchor your heart today. Release every lie you've believed about yourself and let Me remind you who you are—deeply loved, chosen, and forgiven."*

When truth holds you, lies lose their power.

The Belt of Truth is not something we just wear without thought. We need to know God's Word and use it to face every lie. When truth is in place, your armor holds, your footing is steady, and you are ready to stand strong.

Closing Spiritual Seal:

Jesus is your Truth. As you cling to Him and His Word, confusion clears and identity strengthens.

What might change if **His truth held you firm today?**

Application

Write down one specific lie the enemy keeps telling you about your identity or worth. Underneath it, write at least one Bible verse that speaks against that lie (for example: Psalm 139:14, Ephesians 2:10, or 1 John 3:1). Now, take the verse and rewrite it on something you can keep with you: a card you can carry in your wallet, a sticky note on your mirror, or set it as your phone lock-screen for the week. Let this truth become a daily reminder, something you see and touch, anchoring your heart in what God says about you.

Prayer

Father, thank You that Jesus is the Truth and that Your Word is true. Today, I put on the Belt of Truth. Show me every lie I have believed and replace it with how You see me. Keep my heart and mind secure in Your unchanging truth so I can stand confident and free. In Jesus' name, Amen.

Take Up Your Sword

(Speak these aloud)

- I wear the belt of truth. (Ephesians 6:14a)

- God's truth breaks every lie about me. (John 8:32)

- I am God's loved, chosen, and forgiven daughter. (1 John 3:1; Ephesians 1:4; Ephesians 1:7)

- God's truth holds me steady. (Isaiah 33:6; Acts 17:28a)

Journal Prompt

What lie has most often made you question your worth or identity? How does holding on to God's truth change how you see yourself today?

Day 7: The Breastplate of Righteousness – Guarded Hearts

Key Scripture

"...wearing the breastplate of God's righteousness."
Ephesians 6:14b (NLT)

Reflection

Sister, a soldier would never go into battle without a breastplate to protect his vital organs, especially his heart. One direct hit could be deadly. The Bible tells us the same is true for our spiritual lives: "Guard your heart above all else, for it determines the course of your life" (Proverbs 4:23, NLT).

In spiritual battles, the Breastplate of Righteousness protects your heart from some of the enemy's most damaging attacks: accusation, shame, and condemnation. The enemy tries to strike at the core of who you are, bringing up painful memories, past failures, regrets, and every time you felt you didn't measure up. If he can wound your heart with guilt, he can weaken your faith and drain your confidence before God.

But this breastplate has two important and life-giving sides.

First, it is Christ's righteousness, given to you the moment you accepted Jesus. You do not stand before God in your own goodness, because none of us could ever be good enough. You stand in Jesus' perfect righteousness.

When the accuser points out your flaws, you can point to the cross. That truth silences him every time.

Second, the breastplate speaks of a righteous life empowered by the Holy Spirit. It is a daily choice to walk in obedience, integrity, and purity. This is not about earning God's love; it is about living protected. When we obey, we avoid the wounds that sin can cause and keep our hearts soft and open to God.

This is where discernment matters. Conviction leads us to repentance and restoration, while condemnation leads to hiding and despair. The Holy Spirit gently corrects us to bring us closer to God. The enemy condemns us to push us away. The breastplate helps you tell the difference and guard your heart.

For years, early in my faith, I carried a heavy weight of condemnation.

Every mistake in ministry or motherhood felt like proof that I was not worthy to be used by God. I was always waiting for the next accusation. Things changed when the Holy Spirit showed me that the breastplate was not something I had to earn by being perfect. It was a gift already given to me in Jesus. When I started putting on His righteousness each day, shame lost its hold, and my heart began to heal.

When Christ covers your heart, accusation loses its voice.

Sister, protect your heart today. Put on the breastplate. Let Christ's righteousness cover you and let His Spirit help you live it out.

Closing Spiritual Seal

Accusation may come, but it has no power over you. Christ has already called you righteous.

Lean in and hear His whisper:

"My beloved, stand confidently—there is no accusation that can stand against you in My presence. Let Me heal and guard your heart, for you are precious to Me."

Rest in what He has done.

Application

Notice your thoughts today. When guilt or shame comes up, pause and ask yourself:

"Is this conviction from the Holy Spirit leading me to repentance and restoration—or condemnation from the enemy pulling me toward shame and hiding?"

If it is condemnation, speak this truth aloud:

"I am the righteousness of God through Christ Jesus" (2 Corinthians 5:21, NLT).

Prayer

Father God, thank You for covering me with the perfect righteousness of Jesus, which I could never earn, but You freely gave. Today I put on the Breastplate of Righteousness. Protect my heart from every accusation, lie, and wound from the enemy. Quiet the voices of shame and condemnation and help my heart listen to Your truth. Fill me with Your Spirit so I can walk in obedience and integrity. Keep my heart safe, soft, and secure in You. In Jesus' name, amen.

Take Up Your Sword

(Speak these truths aloud)

- I put on righteousness. (Ephesians 6:14b)

- I am righteous in Christ. (2 Corinthians 5:21)

- Shame has no hold on me. (Romans 8:1)

- God guards and heals my heart. (Proverbs 4:23)

Journal Prompt

Where have shame or condemnation tried to hurt your heart lately? How does putting on Christ's righteousness change how you see yourself and that situation today?

Day 8: The Shoes of Peace – Steady and Ready

Key Scripture

"...and with your feet fitted with the readiness
that comes from the gospel of peace."
Ephesians 6:15 (NLT)

Reflection

Sister, let's talk about shoes for a minute. Picture a dusty road under a blazing sun, with the feel of rough leather straps cinched tightly around your ankles. Imagine the sound of sandals scuffing against gritty ground, each step steady and sure as Roman soldiers prepared for whatever lay ahead. As women, we know the right pair of shoes can make or break a day by giving us confidence, keeping us steady, and helping us get where we need to go. Soldiers in Paul's time understood this too. Their sturdy sandals, built for traction and support, kept them from slipping on rough ground and helped them march long distances without stumbling. Wearing the wrong shoes could cost them the battle.

In our spiritual lives, God gives us the perfect shoes: ones fitted with the readiness that comes from the gospel of peace. These shoes do two important things.

First, they give us firm footing. The gospel of peace means the war between you and God is over. Through Jesus, you have been reconciled, forgiven, and brought into right relationship with your Father. This promise of peace has always been central to God's rescue story. Isaiah spoke of the beautiful feet that bring good news, and Jesus calmed storms with a word, showing peace both proclaimed and lived out. When fear, anxiety, or chaos tries to knock you off balance, this peace steadies you. Scripture promises that God's peace "will guard your hearts and minds as you live in Christ Jesus" (Philippians 4:7, NLT). No matter how unstable the ground may feel — whether it is health concerns, family conflict, or uncertainty in the world—His peace gives you traction to stand.

Second, these shoes get you ready to move forward. They prepare you to share the gospel of peace wherever God leads you. One day, I sat beside a friend in a hospital waiting room, the air heavy with worry and prayer. In that solemn space, all I could do was hold her hand, whisper a prayer, and remind her she was not alone. And then, in the hush between our words, peace quietly settled over us, pressing back the tension in the room and lifting the weight from our chests. Another time, over a simple cup of coffee, I listened as a woman poured out her fears about her family. Just listening, offering hope, and gently pointing her back to God's faithfulness brought light, even while nothing had outwardly changed. Whether it is a bedside, a busy café, or a quiet walk in the park, moments like these remind me that when your heart is rooted in God's peace, you are always ready to share that peace with others.

There have been seasons when fear tried to paralyze me and keep me from speaking, stepping out, or trusting God's next assignment. I cried out, "Jesus, I'm afraid. I don't know if I can do this." He gently reminded me, "Daughter, I am with you. You step; I step." With that promise, I intentionally put on these shoes each morning, declaring His peace over my heart, and found the courage to keep moving. The ground stopped shifting beneath me, and I could walk forward with confidence, carrying His message.

God's peace gives you steady footing
and sends you forward with courage.

Sister, let's lace up our shoes together today. As we step forward side by side, may the gospel of peace give us a steady foundation and send us out to bring His light wherever He leads us. **Listen as He whispers**, *"Beloved, you are not alone on this journey. I am with you."*

Closing Spiritual Seal

You stand reconciled and secure in Christ, not by striving but by grace alone. His peace steadies you and flows through you.

Walk with confidence and bring His calm into every room.

Application

Today, whenever fear, anxiety, or unrest rise, pause and place your hand over your heart. As you do, declare aloud:

"I have peace with God through Jesus, and His peace guards my heart and mind."

Then ask the Lord to show you one person who might need that same peace. Reach out with a text, a call, or a simple word of encouragement.

Prayer

Lord, thank You for the gospel of peace that ended the distance between us and brought me back to You forever. I'm especially grateful for a recent moment when You steadied me. Please forgive me for the times I let fear or anxiety throw me off balance.

Today, I put on the shoes of peace. Anchor my heart in Your steady calm. Keep me steady and make me willing and alert to carry Your message of hope wherever You lead me. Let my steps bring Your peace. In the mighty name of Jesus, amen.

Take Up Your Sword

(Speak these truths aloud)

- Today, I choose to put on God's shoes of peace. (Ephesians 6:15)

- Because of Jesus, I have peace with God—nothing can shake me. (Romans 5:1)

- God's peace protects my heart and mind; I am steady and secure. (Philippians 4:7)

- I am ready to share God's peace wherever He leads me. (Ephesians 6:15)

Journal Prompt

Where have fear or anxiety been trying to destabilize you lately? How does knowing you have peace with God—and His peace guarding you—change the way you walk through that situation today?

Day 9: The Shield of Faith — Fire Put Out

"In addition to all of this, take up the shield of faith, with which you can extinguish all the flaming arrows of the evil one."
Ephesians 6:16 (NLT)

Reflection

Often, the enemy launches focused attacks. These are not random, but intentional, meant to destroy your faith, peace, and hope, and to take you out of the fight. These attacks frequently manifest as sudden waves of doubt, fear, temptation, accusation, despair… and even sickness. They can strike without warning and feel overwhelming. Scripture makes it clear: the enemy fires *fiery arrows* designed to burn, disrupt, and destroy. Yet we do not fight as those without hope. At the cross, Jesus took on every weapon of darkness and overcame them through His death and resurrection. The victory of Christ means every arrow the enemy launches is already defeated at its root, and our struggle is now lived out in the confidence of His finished work.

God has not left you exposed. He has given you a powerful defense—the **shield of faith**.

Paul knew exactly what he was describing. A Roman soldier's shield was big enough to cover almost his whole body. It was made to absorb impact and put out flaming arrows as soon as they hit. Imagine the clang of metal as a line of soldiers snapped their shields into place, the intense scent of burning oil as arrows struck and sizzled out, the muffled shouts as each man braced himself behind his shield. When the attacks came, the soldier lifted his shield and trusted the protection it offered. When soldiers stood side by side, their shields locked together, forming a wall that could withstand ongoing attacks.

That is the picture Scripture gives us. **Faith is not just wishing or blind optimism.** It is steadfast trust in God's promises, especially when things look difficult. Imagine being in a doctor's office, waiting for test results, and anxiety starts to rise. Instead of letting fear take over, you remember God's promise to be with you and to work all things for your good. You choose to quietly pray, "Lord, I trust You, whatever comes," even while your heart is pounding. That is raising your shield in a real moment. When the enemy sends arrows of doubt, fear, or accusation, you do not argue with them. Instead, you *raise your shield*. You choose to believe what God has said, even when your feelings or circumstances say otherwise.

This shield was never meant to be carried alone. God calls us to *hold on to hope together*, encourage each other, and stay connected, especially during hard times (see Hebrews 10:23–25). When we join with other believers, our faith grows stronger. Together, we are much less vulnerable to the enemy's attacks.

I have gone through times when the arrows came quickly and fiercely, with fear and lies coming one after another, trying to wear me down. There were occasions when my chest squeezed, and my thoughts spun late into the night — when discouragement felt so heavy it made everything seem gray. I remember how alone I felt in those dark stretches, my prayers sometimes scarcely a whisper. But every time I lifted my shield of faith and spoke God's Word out loud, the attack lost its power. Faith did exactly what God promised it would do.

Sister, do not drop your shield. Pick it up today. As you do, **hear Jesus whisper**, *"Trust Me to shield you from every attack and to fill your heart with My peace."*

Faith does not deny the fire; it raises the shield.

In Christ, every lie loses its burn. **Stand firm and let His faithfulness put out every flaming arrow the enemy sends.**

Closing Spiritual Seal

You were not left exposed in the battle. In Christ, faith covers what the enemy tries to ignite.

Application

Think of one "fiery arrow" the enemy has used against you recently, such as fear, doubt, temptation, accusation, discouragement, or sickness. Find a specific promise from God's Word that speaks directly to it. Write that verse on a card or sticky note and carry it with you for the next 24 hours, pulling it out whenever you feel the attack or need to remember God's faithfulness. Say that promise out loud several times today as you raise your shield of faith.

This practice plants God's truth deeper in your heart and turns promise-hunting into a daily shield.

Prayer

Father, thank You for giving me the shield of faith that extinguishes every fiery arrow the enemy sends. Forgive me for the moments I've lowered my shield and allowed fear or doubt to take hold. Today, I take it up again.

Strengthen my faith to trust Your promises above every lie and attack. Help me stand firm, and surround me with sisters who will stand with me.

Let me pause in silence now, breathing deeply in Your presence, letting Your truth settle into my heart.

In the victorious name of Jesus, Amen.

Take Up Your Sword

(Speak these truths aloud)

- I boldly use the shield of faith, and every attack from the enemy is stopped. (Ephesians 6:16)

- I believe God's promises, even when I feel afraid or things look hard. (Romans 4:20-21)

- Faith protects my heart, my thoughts, and my future. (Philippians 4:7)

- I am safe and protected because I belong to Jesus. (Colossians 3:3)

Journal Prompt

Which fiery arrows have felt strongest for you in this season? What is one next step you will take—before bedtime—to actively trust God in this area? Write down your intention and invite the Lord to strengthen your obedience.

Day 10: The Helmet of Salvation – Protecting Your Mind

Key Scripture

"And take the helmet of salvation..."
Ephesians 6:17a (NLT)

Reflection

Sister, our minds are one of the main places where spiritual battles happen. There is a saying from military strategists that every battle is first won or lost in the mind, and Scripture supports that idea. This battle for our thoughts goes all the way back to the beginning: in Genesis 3, the enemy's first strategy was to plant doubt and confusion in Eve's mind about God's Word and character. From the earliest pages, the mind is shown as the front line where truth or lies take root. Later, Romans 12:2 calls us not to be conformed to the patterns of this world, but to be transformed by the renewing of our minds. A crisis, a diagnosis, a betrayal, or a disappointment may begin on the outside, but it often moves quickly into our minds, where doubt, fear, confusion, or hopelessness try to take root. My husband, Ken, often says, "Take your thoughts captive or they will take you prisoner."

That is why we need to guard this area closely and see our thought life as part of God's bigger redemption story.

The hope of salvation guards your mind
and keeps you secure in Christ.

Paul calls this piece "the hope of salvation" (1 Thessalonians 5:8), and that phrase is important. The Roman soldier's helmet was made to protect the head, the most vulnerable and vital part, from deadly blows. Crafted of heavy bronze or iron and often weighing several pounds, the helmet had cheek guards and a backplate to shield the neck, giving a sense of weight and security in battle. Without a helmet, a soldier could be defeated instantly. With it, he could keep fighting.

The Helmet of Salvation does the same for us. It protects your thoughts from the enemy's attacks of despair, accusation, and fear about what is ahead. The hope of salvation is not just wishful thinking; it is a confident assurance now and a secure expectation for the future. Biblical hope means living with deep assurance today because of what Christ has already accomplished, while also looking forward with unwavering trust to all that God has yet to fulfill.

There have been times in my life when my mind felt under constant pressure, replaying failures, fearing what might happen, and questioning God's promises. Sleepless nights and endless "what if " thoughts made everything harder. The enemy taunted me with, "God is finished with you," and "This trial will destroy you." But when I intentionally put on the Helmet of Salvation—refusing to let my thoughts wander, reminding myself of my identity in Christ, and focusing on what Jesus has done—hope grew stronger. The attacks kept coming, but they no longer had the power to knock me out of the fight.

The helmet is not something we put on just once. We need to take it up every day. As we do, we choose to protect our minds with the sure hope of what Jesus has already done and what He still promises to do.

Sister, protect your precious mind. Put on the helmet. Let the confident hope of your salvation guard your thoughts and strengthen you. **Let the Lord's gentle reminder fill your being:** *"When you focus your mind on Me, I surround you with My protection and peace. Trust that I am always with you, strengthening you and giving you hope—no matter what you face."*

Closing Spiritual Seal

The enemy may attack your thoughts, but the hope of Christ protects your mind when fear and doubt try to come in. In Him, you think from a place of security, not trying to earn it.

Application

Today, if a negative, fearful, or hopeless thought comes into your mind, answer it right away with a truth from His Word about your salvation or situation.

"I am saved by grace."

"Nothing can separate me from the love of God." (Romans 8:38–39)

Say the truth out loud and let it cover your thoughts like a helmet that protects you.

Prayer

Father, thank You for the gift of salvation through Jesus, my sure hope and eternal security. Today, I put on the Helmet of Salvation. Clothe my mind in Your unbreakable strength, surrounding every thought with Your protection. Let Your presence settle over me like a shield, cool and steady, deflecting every lie, doubt, and attack from the enemy. Renew my thoughts with the confidence that I belong to You forever. Take away hopelessness and fill me with joyful assurance based on what Christ has done. Guard my mind and help me keep it focused on You. In the mighty name of Jesus, amen.

Take Up Your Sword

(Speak these truths aloud)

- I take the Helmet of Salvation—my mind is protected. (Ephesians 6:17; 1 Thessalonians 5:8)

- The hope of my salvation guards my thoughts, and no lie can get through. (Romans 15:13; Philippians 4:7)

- I am saved, sealed, and secure in Christ, and nothing can take away my future. (Ephesians 1:13–14; Romans 8:38–39; John 10:28–29)

- My mind is renewed and held steady by the unshakable hope of Jesus. (Romans 12:2; Colossians 3:2–3; Hebrews 6:19)

Journal Prompt

What thoughts have been attacking your mind most persistently lately?

How does the assured hope of your salvation help silence those attacks today?

Day 11: The Sword of the Spirit – Wielding the Word

Key Scripture

"...and take the sword of the Spirit, which is the word of God."
Ephesians 6:17b (NLT)

Reflection

Sister, out of all the pieces of armor God gives us, one is our main weapon: the Sword of the Spirit, which is the Word of God.

Scripture describes it this way:
"For the word of God is alive and powerful. It is sharper than the sharpest two-edged sword..." (Hebrews 4:12, NLT)

Every other piece of armor protects you. The Sword allows you to engage.

But this weapon must be understood rightly.

Spiritual authority is not rooted in volume, intensity, or experience; it is rooted in obedience and submission to God. Obedience, in its simplest form, means choosing God's way even in small, everyday decisions. For example, when you forgive a colleague who has hurt you, even though you would rather hold a grudge, you are practicing obedience. It may also look like honesty when it would be easier to hide the truth, or choosing to speak peace rather than anger in a tense moment. These practical acts of following God's Word, even when they cost us something, strengthen our spiritual lives. Power does not flow from what we have seen or felt; it flows from truth rightly known, believed, and applied.

The Word of God is not something we use to control what happens. It is truth we submit to so Christ can rule our hearts. When we speak Scripture, we are not trying to defeat darkness by force. We are agreeing with what God has already said is true.

That alignment matters.

The enemy knows Scripture. He even quoted it to Jesus in the wilderness, twisting God's Word to try to trick the Son of God (see Matthew 4:1–11).

Jesus did not argue, shout, or rely on experience. He answered with Scripture, spoken in perfect submission to the Father: *"It is written."*

Truth, used the right way, silenced the enemy every time.

The Word is already powerful;
your task is to wield it in faith and obedience.

This is why knowing the Word is essential. The Sword of the Spirit is not decorative—it is not meant to hang unused or be drawn only in moments of crisis. It is meant to be taken up daily, studied, trusted, and spoken from a yielded heart. When God's Word shapes your thinking, guides your choices, and governs your responses, it becomes a powerful instrument in the hands of the Holy Spirit.

Yesterday, we talked about the Helmet of Salvation, which guards the mind. Scripture tells us that our minds are renewed and cleansed through the washing of the Word (Ephesians 5:26). When lies are confronted with truth, confusion gives way to clarity. Fear loosens its grip. Faith finds its footing.

Sister, the Sword of the Spirit is not about spiritual drama; it is about faithful obedience. There is a difference between chasing an emotional high and choosing steady, consistent trust—one may feel exciting, but the quiet path of daily obedience changes everything. It is the even, low-key faithfulness that unleashes genuine spiritual power. When you speak God's Word in humility and trust, heaven backs what aligns with His will. You do not need to make the Word powerful; it already is. Your role is simply to wield it faithfully.

Closing Spiritual Seal

When you speak Scripture in faith, you are not wielding a formula—you are yielding to the Living Word.

His truth confronts every lie, and heaven backs what aligns with Him.

Application

Choose one specific battle you are facing right now. Find two or three Scriptures that directly address that situation. Write them down. Meditate on them. As you speak them aloud throughout the day, pause and take slow, deep breaths with each verse. Let each inhale and exhale anchor the truth of God's Word not only in your mind but in your body. When fear, doubt, or temptation tries to rise, breathe slowly, repeat the Scripture, **pause and let God's truth settle deep within you**, *"Beloved, I have sanctified you with truth, My word is truth."*

Let His promises calm your heart and lead your fight.

Prayer

Father, thank You for giving me the Sword of the Spirit, Your living and powerful Word. Please forgive me for the times I've relied on feelings or experience instead of truth. Today, I take up Your Word with humility and obedience. Teach me to know it, love it, and fully submit to it. Let Your truth shape my mind, guard my heart, and guide my words. I trust You with the outcome as I walk in step with Your will. In the mighty name of Jesus, the Living Word, amen.

Take Up Your Sword

(Speak these truths aloud)

- I take up the Sword of the Spirit—the living Word of God. (Ephesians 6:17; Hebrews 4:12)

- I submit my heart and mind to God's truth; His Word is my authority. (Psalm 119:11; Joshua 1:8)

- I speak Scripture in faith, obedience, and trust—not fear. (2 Corinthians 4:13)

- God's truth governs my thoughts, my words, and my responses. (Psalm 19:14; Psalm 119:105)

Journal Prompt

What situation in your life needs to be brought under the authority of God's Word today? How does knowing that power flows from truth and obedience—not experience—change the way you wield the Sword of the Spirit?

Day 12: Prayer as the Constant Weapon – Tying It All Together

Key Scripture

"And pray in the Spirit on all occasions with all kinds of prayers and requests. With this in mind, be alert and always keep on praying for all the Lord's people."
Ephesians 6:18 (NLT)

Reflection

Sister, we've explored each part of God's armor, learning what it is, how it protects us, and how it helps us stand strong. But Paul does not end with the sword. He shows us the one thing that brings the whole armor to life and keeps it working: prayer.

Let me share a story. When I was struggling with anxiety, I would put on the Belt of Truth in my mind and remind myself of God's promises, but fear still lingered. One day, I began praying over those promises, asking God to let His truth break through my worry. In that moment of honest prayer, I felt peace settle over me in a way I had not before. It was as if prayer unlocked the power of truth and actually guarded my heart. That showed me prayer does not just keep us close to God—it activates the protection He has already given us.

Prayer keeps the armor alive and your heart connected
to the One who fights for you.

Praying in the Spirit at all times, with all kinds of prayers, is what holds the armor together and keeps it secure. It helps us stay alert to the enemy's tricks, stay close to God, and keep going when things get hard. Prayer is not just an extra step or something to do later; it is how we connect with God and find strength as we stand firm.

Let's pause for a moment and put this into practice. Take a slow, deep breath in, focusing your mind on Jesus. As you breathe out, quietly say, "Lord, I am here with You." Repeat this simple breath and prayer for about 30 seconds. Let any tension ease away as you sense His presence. Notice how even this small practice shifts your awareness and helps you stand quietly but firmly in God's strength.

Prayer keeps us in the right place. It softens our hearts, sharpens our minds, and reminds us to depend on the Lord. When we pray, we do not just put on the armor; we stay close to the One who gives it to us. Prayer is more than us speaking—it is a two-way conversation where God also responds. Take a moment to think: How has God spoken back to you, comforted you, or guided you when you have prayed?

Today, let's make prayer a regular part of your day. Here is a simple daily prayer to help you put on the full armor of God. Say it out loud each morning or listen to the companion audio. Let it be both your battle cry and your love song to Jesus.

Daily Armor Prayer

Father God, I thank You for the full armor You have given me in Christ.
Today I put on the Belt of Truth—Jesus, gird me with Your unchanging Word.
I put on the Breastplate of Righteousness—Jesus, cover my heart with Your perfection.
I fit my feet with the Shoes of Peace—Jesus, steady me and send me with Your gospel.
I take up the Shield of Faith—Jesus, let Your faithfulness extinguish every fiery arrow.
I take the Helmet of Salvation—Jesus, guard my mind with the hope of my eternal security.
I lift the Sword of the Spirit—Jesus, the Living Word, speak through me and cut through every lie.
And I pray in the Spirit on all occasions, staying alert and persistent.
Clothe me fully, Lord. I stand ready in You.
In the mighty name of Jesus, amen.

Closing Spiritual Seal

Stay connected, keep listening, and be ready to respond. When you keep talking with God, you never have to fight alone.

Application

Try praying the Daily Armor Prayer out loud every morning this week. As you pray, pause after each part and ask the Holy Spirit to show you a personal need—maybe for your family, your struggles, or for others. Let prayer be a real conversation, not just a list to get through. Also, today, think of one person you can text and simply say, "I'm praying for you."

As we pray for each other, we remind one another that we stand together and never have to face the battle alone.

Prayer

Lord, teach me to pray without ceasing. Thank You for the privilege of coming boldly into Your presence. Through prayer, keep every piece of armor active and secure in my life. Help me stay alert, persistent, and deeply connected to You. Let my prayers align with Your will, strengthen my sisters, and advance Your Kingdom. "Let everything that has breath praise the Lord" (Psalm 150:6). In Jesus' name, amen.

Take time to make space for Jesus to speak to you. Right now, after you have finished your prayer, sit silent for a moment or two. Sit quietly, breathe slowly, and listen for His gentle voice. Notice any word, image, or feeling that comes to your heart. Let this silence be a space where you listen as much as you speak.

Take Up Your Sword

(Speak these truths aloud)

- Because I pray in the Spirit on all occasions, my armor is secure and effective today. (Ephesians 6:18)

- Because I stay alert and connected to God, I know I do not fight alone. (Joshua 1:9; Hebrews 13:5-6)

- As I pray and trust God's will, I am strengthened and sustained for whatever comes. (Philippians 4:6-7; Isaiah 40:31)

- Through constant prayer, I am fully clothed in Christ and walk in holy confidence. (Romans 13:14; Hebrews 4:16)

Journal Prompt

How has praying, or not praying, changed how steady you feel spiritually lately? What is one thing you want to bring to God regularly this week? When you paused earlier to give space for Jesus to speak to you, did any word, image, or feeling come to your heart?

MOVEMENT II:

CLOTHED IN CHRIST

In the first movement, we stood with Scripture and considered the Armor of God as God first revealed it—clear, sacred, and necessary. But armor was never meant to remain an idea studied from afar. *It was meant to be worn.*

This second movement invites you deeper—not into more striving, but into deeper union.

Here, we move from learning *what* the armor is to beholding *who* the armor is. Scripture reveals these pieces not as tools we manage, but as a life we inhabit. Truth is a Person. Righteousness is a covering. Peace, faith, salvation, and the Word are Christ Himself living in us.

Many women know this place of quiet weariness. They pray faithfully. They resist and rebuke. Yet without intimacy, identity, and abiding, warfare grows heavy. Here, the Lord gently releases the grip of performance and calls us back to the simplicity of remaining in Him.

- Here, authority flows from belonging.

- Victory flows from union.

- Strength flows from abiding.

You are not learning to fight harder.
You are learning to live more deeply clothed.

In Judges 6–8, Gideon is chosen by God for a task far bigger than himself. But Gideon does not respond with bold confidence. He responds with fear, questions, and a deep sense of inadequacy. He sees his weakness clearly, yet God does not answer him with frustration. The Father responds with patience, reassurance, and grace, even meeting Gideon in the signs he asks for. Then Judges 6:34 gives us a powerful image: "the Spirit of the Lord clothed

Gideon." The Hebrew word, **lābash**, means **to clothe, dress, or wrap oneself in a garment**. The picture is striking. The Lord did not merely stand near Gideon; He wrapped Himself around him. Gideon was no longer facing the calling in his own frailty. He was covered by the Spirit of God. In the same way, when we are clothed in Christ, we do not stand in our own righteousness. We stand covered, secured, and made ready in Him.

Let the Holy Spirit shift your posture—from striving to resting, from effort to trust, from managing battles to walking in nearness. This is where warfare becomes sustainable, peace becomes anchored, identity unshakable.

You are not putting something on.
You are clothed. You are covered.
You are living from Someone within.

Day 13: Clothed in Christ — The True Armor

Key Scripture

"For all of you who were baptized into Christ have clothed yourselves with Christ."
Galatians 3:27 (NLT)

Reflection

Sister, over the past days we've learned each piece of God's armor—how to put them on, how they protect us, how they help us stand strong. Today, we go deeper. The armor isn't just separate tools we manage. It is Jesus Himself.

Every piece points to Jesus. When we put on the full armor of God, we are truly clothing ourselves with Christ. Paul urged first-century believers, "Clothe yourselves with the Lord Jesus Christ" (Romans 13:14). For his Roman and Galatian readers, clothing marked identity—what you wore showed who you belonged to. By telling believers to put on Christ, Paul called them to find their ultimate identity in Him above status, background, or tradition. The armor is not separate from Him. It is an invitation to stay close and let Him be everything we need.

Consider this:

- The Belt of Truth? Jesus is the Truth.

- The Breastplate of Righteousness? Jesus is our Righteousness.

- The Shoes of Peace? Jesus is the Prince of Peace.

- The Shield of Faith? Jesus is the Author and Perfecter of our faith.

- The Helmet of Salvation? Jesus is the Hope of our salvation.

- The Sword of the Spirit? Jesus is the Living Word.

When we put on the armor, we put on Jesus. We hide ourselves in Him and let Him cover every weak spot. We don't win by trying harder to use the armor rightly, but by staying close to the One who *is* our armor.

Self-effort exhausts us, but Spirit-dependence sets us free.

Abiding in Christ doesn't mean we step away from battle. It means we face it together with Him, not by our own strength.

I've shared this truth for years and seen it change lives, including mine. When we stop fighting alone and simply say, "Lord Jesus, I clothe myself in You today," everything shifts. Fear loses its hold. Shame fades. Accusations lose power. Suffering may not leave, but we are carried through it, safe in Christ.

You don't wear armor. You wear Jesus.

Sister, this is victory's real secret: it is not just wearing armor but wearing Jesus Himself.

Feel His presence and listen: *"Abide in Me as I abide in you. Stand firm and walk in the victory I have already won for you. When you live hidden in Me, you are secure, steadfast, and victorious—no matter what comes. Trust Me to sustain you, My beloved daughter, for I am with you always."*

Closing Spiritual Seal

You are not protected because you tried harder. You are protected because you are *in Christ*. Victory comes from staying close to Him, not working harder. We face every battle together with Him.

Application

Take a quiet moment now. Before speaking this prayer aloud, pause for thirty seconds.

Breathe in, silently saying, "Christ in me." Breathe out, "I in Christ."

Let your heart settle into this truth, then pray:

Prayer

"Lord Jesus, I clothe myself with You today. Be my Truth, my Righteousness, my Peace, my Faith, my Salvation, and my Word. I abide in You, and You abide in me. Today I choose to stop striving and start abiding. Clothe me completely in Yourself and cover every part of me with who You are. Let me face every battle hidden in You, resting in You, drawing every breath from You. I put You on as my everything. In Your precious name, amen."

Let this prayer become part of your daily armor routine.

Take Up Your Sword

(Speak these truths aloud)

- Today, I put on Jesus—He is my armor. (Romans 13:14; Galatians 3:27; Ephesians 6:10-11)

- Jesus, You are my Truth, Righteousness, and Peace. I am secure in You. (John 14:6; 1 Corinthians 1:30; Ephesians 2:14)

- I abide in You, Jesus, and You in me. I stand firm in Your victory. (John 15:4; 1 John 4:13; 1 Corinthians 15:57)

- Hidden in You, Jesus, I am secure, steadfast, and victorious. (Colossians 3:3; Psalm 91:1; Romans 8:37)

Journal Prompt

How does seeing the armor as clothing yourself in Jesus—not separate pieces to manage—change things? How does abiding in Christ, instead of your own strength, change how you face today's battles? What is one concrete step you'll take tomorrow to remain clothed in Him?

Day 14: Jesus – Our Truth

Key Scripture

"Stand your ground, putting on the belt of truth..."
Ephesians 6:14a (NLT)

Reflection

Sister, have you ever felt so confused that a lie seemed completely true? I have—and I know many of you have too.

One evening I sat alone on my back porch, wooden boards cool beneath me, crickets singing steady in the deepening dark. My hands gripped the chair, knuckles tight with worry. Prayers slipped out as whispers while doubts circled my mind beneath the night sky.

Even those who love Jesus deeply face these battles—confusion, fear, shame, exhaustion. Faith doesn't make us immune. But right there, in the struggle, God meets us.

When we put on the **Belt of Truth,** we do more than hold our armor together. We clothe ourselves with Jesus Himself—the Way, the Truth, and the Life. To be clothed in Christ means letting His truth surround and shape our thoughts, identity, and circumstances.

The enemy twists reality, plants deception, showing just enough truth to make lies believable. That's why Scripture calls us to be taught, led, and transformed by God's truth:

"You will know the truth, and the truth will set you free." (John 8:32)

"Sanctify them by Your truth. Your word is truth." (John 17:17)

Facts describe what we see in the moment.
Truth declares what God says is ultimately real.

I learned this when watching my son Brandon struggle with heroin addiction. Every parent's nightmare became my reality—deep grief, constant questions, aching helplessness. One day he looked at me and said, "Mom, addicts don't change. They die or go to prison."

My heart broke. The facts seemed to confirm his words. But something rose up inside me that refused to agree.

"I cannot hear that," I said through tears. "I refuse to hear that."

Later, I fell before God: *"Lord, the fact is my son is an addict, but the Truth is greater. Whom the Son sets free is free indeed."* (John 8:36)

Facts describe circumstances. Truth declares God's reality.

The fact might be a diagnosis—Truth says Jesus carried our sickness (Isaiah 53:5).

The fact might be an empty bank account—Truth says God supplies all our needs (Philippians 4:19).

Our daughter Tiffany experienced this when traveling cross-country to ministry school with little money and no place to live. During her Denver layover, anxiety wrestling hope, her phone rang.

"An apartment is waiting for you."

Tears fell as God's provision—timely, personal, unmistakable—proved truth greater than facts.

When we clothe ourselves in Jesus—the Truth—lies lose their power.

Sister, today stand firm, anchored in the One who is Truth itself.

Closing Spiritual Seal

You are held by Truth Himself. Lies may whisper, but they cannot define what only God declares.

Application

Think of one lie the enemy whispers about your identity, family, or future. Notice when it appears and how your body responds—tight stomach? Racing heart? Heavy chest?

Identify the *fact* making that lie believable.

Find one Scripture speaking God's truth into it.

Declare it out loud today. Every time the lie returns, speak truth again.

Prayer

Lord Jesus, You are my Truth. Today I clothe myself in You. Lead me in Your truth, teach me, make me holy by Your Word. Show me every lie I've believed and replace it with Your truth. Help me trust Your Word above every circumstance. In Your mighty name, amen.

Take Up Your Sword

(Speak these truths aloud)

- I am clothed in Jesus and lies have no power over me. (Galatians 3:27; 2 Corinthians 10:4–5)

- I know the Truth, and the Truth sets me free. (John 8:32; John 8:36)

- God's truth is greater than any fact. (John 17:17; Isaiah 55:11)

- I am strengthened by God's Word. (Ephesians 6:14)

Journal Prompt

What "fact" does Jesus want to speak His truth over today? How does clothing yourself in Jesus—the Truth—bring hope to that situation?

Day 15: Jesus - Our Righteousness

Key Scripture

"...and the body armor of God's righteousness."
Ephesians 6:14b (NLT)

Reflection

Sister, when we put on the Breastplate of Righteousness, we're not trying to improve ourselves to earn God's approval. We're covering ourselves with Jesus, who *is* our Righteousness.

The enemy attacks the heart with accusation and shame, whispering reminders of every failure, regret, and moment we fell short. His goal? Make you believe your standing with God depends on your performance.

But here's the glorious gospel truth: Jesus became our righteousness.

The moment you trusted Him, God exchanged your sin for Christ's perfection.

I sometimes teach it like this: Jesus put on a "man-suit" so we could wear a "God-suit."

We don't become God, but we're fully covered in His righteousness with His perfect standing before the Father.

Scripture declares:

"For God made Christ, who never sinned, to be the offering for our sin, so that we could be made right with God through Christ." (2 Corinthians 5:21)

"I am overwhelmed with joy in the LORD my God! For he has dressed me with the clothing of salvation and draped me in a robe of righteousness." (Isaiah 61:10)

Imagine slipping into Christ's righteousness—soft, radiant, wrapping you like protective garment. Where accusation once pierced, His purity now shields your soul.

Picture walking into an important meeting, anxiety rising, heart thumping with fear, past mistakes whispering you're not enough. You pause and declare, *"Jesus is my Righteousness. I am clothed in His perfection."*

Jesus did more than improve you. He covered you.

Fear loosens. Peace steadies.

You stand before God—not in fear, but confident joy—hidden in Christ. I know condemnation's weight. One night, Bible open on my bed's edge, heavy with regret over undoable mistakes, my eyes fell on 2 Corinthians 5:21.

Truth broke through: *Jesus really is my righteousness.*

I whispered, *"You are enough, Jesus. You have covered me."* Peace washed over me. I stopped earning what He'd already given and rested in His covering. The enemy's shame-arrows still come, but they fall powerless at Jesus' feet.

At this moment, hear Jesus remind your heart: *"Beloved, you are secure and accepted because of what I have done for you."*

Sister, put on Jesus today. Let His righteousness guard your heart. You stand accepted before God.

Closing Spiritual Seal

You don't stand before God by performance, but by Christ's perfection.

Righteousness isn't achieved. It's Someone you wear.

Application

When accusation rises today, refuse it. Declare aloud:

"Jesus is my Righteousness. I am clothed in His perfection."

Choose one Scripture above. Speak it throughout the day until truth settles deep.

Prayer

Lord Jesus, my Righteousness, today I clothe myself in You. Thank You for taking on humanity so I could wear Your righteousness. Every accusation silenced, every shame-wound healed at the cross. I stand accepted, secure before the Father. Fill me with Your Spirit to walk in what You've given. Today I rest in Your finished work. In Your precious name, amen.

Take Up Your Sword

(Speak these truths aloud)

- Jesus is my righteousness and covers me completely. (1 Corinthians 1:30)

- No condemnation for those in Christ Jesus. (Romans 8:1)

- The Lord Himself is my righteousness. (Jeremiah 23:6)

- Clothed in Christ's robe of righteousness. (Isaiah 61:10; 2 Corinthians 5:21)

Journal Prompt

Where has the enemy accused or shamed you? How does clothing yourself in Jesus—your Righteousness—change how you see yourself and your situation today?

Day 16: Jesus — Our Peace

Key Scripture

"...and with your feet fitted with the readiness that comes from the gospel of peace."
Ephesians 6:15 (NLT)

Reflection

Sister, have you ever been around someone whose anxiety felt like a heavy cloud? Sometimes just being near them makes you anxious too. I've been that person more times than I'd like to admit.

One morning at my kitchen table, heart pounding, mind racing with the day ahead, my clipped words spilled anxiety onto my family before I even realized it. Maybe you've been there—carrying tension you wish you could leave behind, longing for peace but unsure how to grab it.

Peace isn't found. It's worn.

In today's world, peace is the greatest treasure. The enemy steals it with anxiety, discouragement, unrest. Without peace, hearts unsettle, focus drifts.

But here's the life-changing truth: when we put on the shoes of the gospel of peace, we're putting on a Person.

Jesus is our Peace.

His peace anchors you—steady and calm inside even when life swirls.

Scripture declares:

"For Christ himself has brought peace to us..." (Ephesians 2:14)

"Since we have been made right in God's sight by faith, we have peace with God..." (Romans 5:1)

This peace isn't circumstantial. It's rooted in reconciliation with God through Christ's sacrifice. The war between you and God is over. You're forgiven, accepted, brought near.

Jesus promised: *"I am leaving you with a gift—peace of mind and heart... Don't be troubled or afraid."* (John 14:27)

He never promised trouble-free lives. *"Here on earth, you will have many trials..."* But then: *"Take heart, because I have overcome the world."* (John 16:33)

What trial faces you now? His promise isn't escaping the storm but walking through it with Him beside you.

When we declare, *"Lord Jesus, You are my Peace,"* everywhere we go becomes opportunity to carry His calm—into tense meetings, checkout lines, stressed moments with children.

I've seen this transformation. Before learning to clothe myself in Jesus as Prince of Peace, disruptions sent me spiraling. But there have been seasons since when chaos swirled around me, yet I walked steadily. His peace didn't remove challenges—it anchored my heart through them, quietly overflowing to calm what fear once ruled.

If God transformed my panic into steady confidence, He can do the same for you.

Sister, put on your shoes today. Let Jesus—Prince of Peace—steady your steps and send you carrying His peace.

Closing Spiritual Seal

Peace does not mean the absence of trouble. It means Christ is with you in the middle of it.

Listen for His quiet voice above the noise, saying, *"Stay close to Me; remember that My promises are true and My presence is your greatest protection. You are safe in Me—rest here, beloved."*

Application

When anxiety or unrest rises today—whether in you or around you—pause and declare aloud:

"Jesus is my Peace. I have peace with God through Him."

Then ask the Lord to show you one person or place where you can carry His peace today.

Prayer

Lord Jesus, my Prince of Peace, I put on Your peace today.

Thank You for reconciling me to God and giving me a peace the world cannot give or take away. Let the peace of Christ rule in my heart. Steady me when life feels chaotic, guard my heart when anxiety rises, and help me carry Your calm wherever I go.

Let every place I walk reflect Your presence. In Your mighty name, Amen.

Take Up Your Sword

(Speak these truths aloud)

- Jesus is my Prince of Peace, and His peace rules my heart. (Isaiah 9:6; Ephesians 2:14)

- I have peace with God through Christ, and nothing can take it away. (Romans 5:1; John 10:28–29)

- Jesus gives me His peace, not the world's. I walk steady and unafraid. (John 14:27; John 16:33)

- Wherever I go, I carry the gospel of peace. God's presence brings calm and hope. (Romans 15:13; Matthew 5:9)

Journal Prompt

Where has the enemy tried to steal your peace lately?

How does clothing yourself in Jesus—the Prince of Peace—and trusting His promises change the way you face that situation today?

Day 17: Jesus – Our Faith

Key Scripture

"In addition to all this, take up the shield of faith, with which you can extinguish all the flaming arrows of the evil one."
Ephesians 6:16 (NLT)

Reflection

Sister, faith isn't optimism or positive thinking. Faith is choosing to trust Jesus—who He is, what He's done, what He's promised.

Scripture says Jesus is *"the author and finisher of our faith"* (Hebrews 12:2). He begins it, sustains it, completes it.

"The life I now live in the flesh I live by faith in the Son of God, who loved me and gave Himself for me." (Galatians 2:20)

Each time we choose faith, we clothe ourselves in Christ again—His life, victory, faithfulness covering us.

Faith doesn't ignore the fire. It raises the shield.

Picture stepping into a difficult meeting or situation. Quietly remind yourself: *"I live by faith in the Son of God."* Let Jesus' faithfulness be what you wear.

When fiery arrows hit—sickness, lies, fear, despair—you feel them: stomach knotting, thoughts racing, heart heavy.

Lifting the shield means declaring: *"I trust who Jesus is and what He's promised, even when it's hard."*

The shield places Christ between you and attack. His promises meet arrows before they wound.

I've walked seasons of relentless attacks. One of the hardest: devastating news from someone I love—words like a death sentence over something precious. Facts screamed hopeless.

Just like before, immediately said, **"I can't hear that."** Not ignoring reality but refusing hopelessness' final word over God's promise.

My husband and I stood on Scripture, spoke life, trusted the Author of faith to finish what He'd started. By God's grace, we saw His victory.

When circumstances scream hopelessness, faith refuses to let it have final word.

Abraham trusted impossible promises. Daniel's friends stood in fire believing God's faithfulness. Again and again, God's people were protected not by their strength, but His.

That same faithfulness surrounds you today.

Pause and hear His whisper: *"I began your faith, and I will finish it."*

Sister, when arrows come, lift your shield. Clothe yourself in Jesus, the Faithful One.

Closing Spiritual Seal

You're not protected by your faith's strength, but Christ's faithfulness.

Stand behind His promises today.

Application

Name one fiery arrow aimed at you now—lie, fear, accusation. Find Scripture revealing who Jesus is/what He's promised. Speak it aloud today until the flame dies.

Prayer

Lord Jesus, Author and Finisher of my faith, I clothe myself in You today. Thank You for loving me, living in me, giving Yourself for me. When arrows come, help me lift faith's shield—trusting who You are, what You've done, what You've promised. Let Your faithfulness cover me. In Your mighty name, amen.

Take Up Your Sword

(Speak these truths aloud)

- Jesus authors and finishes my faith. His faithfulness shields me. (Hebrews 12:2; Psalm 91:4)

- I live by faith in the Son of God who lives in me. (Galatians 2:20)

- God's promises are yes and amen in Christ. (2 Corinthians 1:20)

- I stand covered, victorious through Christ. (Romans 8:37; Ephesians 6:16)

Journal Prompt

What fiery arrow targets you now? How does clothing yourself in Jesus—Author of your faith—help lift your shield today? Tonight, write one sentence: how did your shield hold? What do you trust God for tomorrow?

Day 18: Jesus - Our Salvation

Key Scripture

"And take the helmet of salvation..."
Ephesians 6:17a (NLT)

Reflection

Sister, every temptation, struggle, and stronghold begins with a thought.

You can't stop birds from flying overhead, but you can stop them from building nests there.

The hope of salvation is not wishful thinking. It is confident assurance.

Thoughts may come uninvited, but you're not powerless. When heavy thoughts swoop in, pause and answer with truth aloud:

"I have the mind of Christ."

"My thoughts are guarded by God's peace." (Philippians 4:7)

Paul calls this helmet "the hope of salvation" (1 Thessalonians 5:8). The Roman *galea* — bronze or iron — protected the head, deflected blows, identified the soldier's army.

Our Helmet does the same: protecting from hopelessness, future fears, identity doubts. You're saved, sealed, held by Jesus — living the "already/not yet." Fully saved now, yet anticipating completion.

When the enemy whispers *"You're too far gone"* or *"God is finished with you,"* the helmet declares: *My salvation is secure in Christ.*

Gospel hope isn't positive thinking (better outcomes). It's the mind of Christ — anchored in His finished work.

I've felt my mind under attack—replaying hurts until hopelessness threatened to drown me. Like a current pulling me from shore. But through choosing the Helmet—refusing wandering thoughts, speaking who I am in Christ, clinging to Jesus' done work—hope returned.

Victory came quietly: peaceful evenings, shorter worry spirals. God renewing my mind, moment by moment.

When we wrap ourselves in Jesus, Hope of Salvation — His finished work — not our emotions — determines truth.

Lean into His reassurance: *"Daughter, when worry rises and hurts return, remember I am with you. My hope is steady, My victory secure. Let Me renew your mind today."*

Sister, guard your beautiful mind. Put on the helmet. Let salvation's hope steady your heart.

Closing Spiritual Seal

Your salvation is secure. Christ's hope protects when dark thoughts come. Stand steady — your future is safe in Him.

Application

When negative thoughts hit today, answer immediately. Place your hand on your head and speak truth aloud:

"I am saved by grace."

"Nothing separates me from God's love." (Romans 8:38–39)

Prayer

Father, thank You for salvation through Jesus — my sure hope, eternal security. Today I put on the Helmet of Salvation. Guard my mind from lies, doubt, enemy attacks. Fill my thoughts with confidence I belong to You forever.

Quiet hopelessness. Remind me of Christ's victory. Cover my sisters fighting mind battles — remind them they're not alone. In Jesus' name, amen.

Take Up Your Sword

(Speak these truths aloud)

- Jesus, Hope of Salvation, guards my mind. (Ephesians 6:17; 1 Thessalonians 5:8)

- My salvation is secure—nothing takes it away. (Ephesians 1:13–14; John 10:28)

- Christ's hope renews my mind, steady and sure. (Romans 12:2; Hebrews 6:19)

- Hidden in Christ, my future secure forever. (Colossians 3:3; Romans 8:38–39)

Journal Prompt

What thought attacks your mind most? How does Jesus — your Salvation — steady you today?

Day 19: Jesus - the Word

"...and the sword of the Spirit, which is the word of God."
Ephesians 6:17b (NLT)

Reflection

Sister, taking up the Sword of the Spirit means clothing yourself in Jesus Himself. When you speak the written Word in faith, it becomes the Living Word—Christ—confronting the enemy through you.

Scripture pictures this:

"He made my mouth like a sharpened sword." (Isaiah 49:2)

"Let the praises of God be in their mouths, and a sharp sword in their hands." (Psalm 149:6)

John reveals the mystery:

"In the beginning was the Word... The Word became flesh." (John 1:1,14)

"His name is called The Word of God." (Revelation 19:13)

Jesus—the eternal Word—walked dusty roads, heard children's laughter, smelled baking bread. God didn't stay distant. He moved into our world.

"When His Word lives in you, you are living in Him—and heaven responds."

Every promise reveals who He is. Because you're beloved, adopted, righteous in Christ, you stand in His authority.

Yesterday's Helmet protected our minds. Today the Word renews them—like standing beneath truth's waterfall, lies and anxiety rinsing away.

Picture your thoughts soaking in Scripture now. Fear loosens. Christ's truth rises from your heart, speaks through your mouth.

Jesus said: *"If you abide in Me, and My words abide in you..."* (John 15:7)

When you pray from *His* heart, not just yours, prayers transform: *"Lord, let love guide my words."*

Speaking Scripture isn't formulaic magic. It's living conversation with Jesus.

Mechanical repetition grows lifeless. Heart-connected truth cuts through deception.

The enemy cannot stand the Living Word.

I saw this when heaviness settled over our home like fog. Discouragement crept in. I couldn't shake it. I began speaking Scripture aloud daily—not as technique, but inviting Jesus, the Living Word, to rule our atmosphere.

Within days, heaviness lifted. Peace returned. Doors opened.

It wasn't my words. It was Jesus speaking through me.

Sister, pick up your sword. Clothe yourself in Jesus, the Living Word.

Closing Spiritual Seal

When you speak God's Word in faith, Christ stands with you.

Abide in Him.

Let His Word fight.

Application

Choose one promise for your current battle. Meditate until you see Jesus in it. Speak it aloud today—as conversation with your Living Savior.

Prayer

Lord Jesus, Living Word, I clothe myself in You. Let Your Word live deeply in me. Wash my mind, renew my thoughts, fill my mouth with truth.

Speak to me now. When attacks come, let Your voice cut through lies. Fight for me, through me today. In your powerful name, Amen.

Take Up Your Sword

(Speak these truths aloud)

- I clothe myself in Jesus, the Living Word. (John 1:1,14; Revelation 19:13)

- God's Word alive, powerful. (Hebrews 4:12)

- I abide in Christ, His Word in me. (John 15:7)

- Speaking truth, enemy loses ground. (Matthew 4:1–11; Ephesians 6:17)

Journal Prompt

What battle needs Jesus, the Living Word?

How does speaking Scripture as conversation change your approach? What breakthrough will you record tonight?

SECTION III:

ADVANCING WITH STEADFASTNESS

When clothed in Christ, you don't retreat. You advance—one sure step at a time—feeling solid ground beneath as you press forward.

In this final movement, we shift from *learning* the armor to *living* it. Battle doesn't end with understanding or breakthrough moments. It continues through daily faithfulness—at home, in relationships, calling, long obedience-seasons where feelings fade but footing holds.

Here, spiritual warfare becomes less dramatic, more enduring. Victory shines not just in breakthroughs, but in rooted, peaceful faithfulness over time.

The armor—Christ Himself—equips this steadfastness:

- **Belt of truth** grounds you in the real, unchanging.

- **Breastplate of righteousness** guards against shame, accusation.

- **Shoes of peace** steady uneven steps.

- **Shield of faith** extinguishes doubt, fear.

- **Helmet of salvation** protects with Christ's hope.

- **Sword of the Spirit** empowers truthful speech, firm standing.

Each piece *is* Christ—your Truth, Righteousness, Peace, Faith, Salvation, Living Word. You advance not by your strength, but because Christ goes before, beside, within.

I remember a particularly intense season when a friend shared a simple word of encouragement from the Lord with me: *"I am with you"*, Yet after receiving that word, the battle only intensified. One day I was walking in my neighborhood when the weight of it all broke through. I stopped in the middle of the road and cried out in anguish, *"Where are You? You said You are with me, but I can't feel You."*

Looking back now, I know something I could not see in that moment: Jesus was not only with me—He was carrying me. I could never have made it through on my own strength.

This is the heart of steadfastness: trusting that Christ is holding you, even when you feel weak and weary.

As you enter these final days, remember this:

You are not racing to the finish line. You are learning, step by step, like a toddler taking uncertain first steps—wobbly, reaching for something steady, yet always moving forward in delight—how to keep your footing in the victory that is already yours.

When the enemy whispers that you are failing, remember this truth:

You are not fighting for victory—you are standing in the victory Christ has already won.

This is what it means to advance with steadfastness: rooted, faithful, and unafraid.

Call to Action

As you move into these final days, ask the Lord to show you where He is carrying you and how He is teaching you to stand firm in His strength.

Day 20: Releasing Offense – Guarding Against the Root of Bitterness

Key Scripture

Hebrews 12:15 (NLT)

Reflection

Sister, offense is one of the enemy's most subtle and effective traps.

The enemy often whispers thoughts like, *"They will never change,"* or *"You deserve better,"* or *"This always happens to you."* These quiet thoughts can feel justified—even reasonable—but their purpose is always the same: to pull us away from grace and trap us in unforgiveness.

When offense takes hold, something shifts inside us. Prayer turns into withdrawal. Intercession turns into replaying the hurt. Instead of trusting God with our pain, we hold onto it.

Over time, resentment grows beneath the surface, becoming what Scripture calls a poisonous root of bitterness.

Hebrews 12:15 warns us to watch carefully for that root. God is not harsh in this warning; He is protective. Bitterness blocks the free flow of His grace in our hearts and relationships.

And bitterness never stays contained.

It spreads into marriages, parenting, friendships, ministries, and even our joy. Before it harms anyone else, it poisons us. It can affect not only our spiritual lives, but also our minds and bodies.

This is where forgiveness becomes essential—and where confusion often arises.

Forgiveness is not a feeling.
It is a choice.

It is an act of obedience made possible by grace, not simply an emotional response to healing. You may still feel hurt, disappointed, or wounded, but you can still choose to forgive.

If we wait until we feel forgiving, offense keeps its grip. When we choose forgiveness, the enemy loses his foothold.

But forgiveness is not the same as reconciliation.

You can release someone in your heart and forgive them even when trust has been broken or a relationship cannot safely be restored. Forgiveness happens inside you. Rebuilding trust may take time—and sometimes it is not possible, especially when safety is involved.

Scripture calls us to this freedom:

"Get rid of all bitterness, rage, anger, harsh words, and slander... Instead, be kind to each other, tenderhearted, forgiving one another, just as God through Christ has forgiven you." **Ephesians 4:31–32**

Choosing forgiveness does not minimize what happened, excuse sin, or remove healthy boundaries. It simply places the offense in God's hands and removes the enemy's claim on your heart.

Healing may take time.

But forgiveness is a decision you can make today. Sometimes you may need to make it again and again.

I have experienced this in my own life.

There were seasons when offense tried to take root through deep hurts and betrayal. I remember carrying anger for weeks, feeling it like a tight knot in my stomach that would not loosen.

But when I chose to forgive—before my feelings changed—something shifted.

That knot began to release. The anger dissolved.

The root began to wither. Grace returned.

Peace followed. Freedom came.

Perhaps Jesus is whispering to your heart today:

"Release your grip on resentment, beloved, and allow My forgiveness to flow through you. As I have freely forgiven you, let My love soften your heart so you can forgive others and walk in true freedom with Me."

Sister, don't let offense trap you.

Guard your heart. Choose forgiveness.

Keep standing in the gap—free, grounded, and unentangled.

Closing Spiritual Seal

Forgiveness is not about what you feel—it is about what you choose.

When you release offense, you protect the flow of God's grace in your heart. The enemy loses his foothold, and freedom begins to grow where bitterness once tried to take root.

Application

Before you begin, pause for a moment.

Take a slow, deep breath in and gently release it. Invite the Holy Spirit into this moment and allow your heart to quiet before Him.

Now think of one offense you may be carrying, whether large or small. Write down the person's name and the hurt you have been holding onto.

Then pray this prayer of release:

"Lord, I choose to forgive [name] as You have forgiven me. I place this hurt in Your hands and ask You to pull up any root of bitterness in my heart."

When you finish, tear up the paper or discard it as a symbol of release and freedom.

Prayer

Father, thank You for showing me the danger of bitterness and the freedom found in forgiveness. Today I choose to forgive—not by my strength, but by Your grace.

Forgive me for holding onto offense, and help me release every hurt to You. Pull up every root of bitterness and fill my heart with Your peace, love, and grace.

I forgive as You have forgiven me. In the mighty name of Jesus, Amen.

Take Up Your Sword

(Speak these truths aloud)

- Forgiveness is my choice, not my feeling, and I choose it today. *(Ephesians 4:31–32; Colossians 3:13)*

- Every root of bitterness is pulled up; God's grace flows freely in me. *(Hebrews 12:15; James 4:6)*

- I forgive as Christ forgave me—by His power and for His glory. *(Ephesians 4:32; Colossians 3:13)*

- I stand in the gap with love and prayer; the enemy's trap is broken. *(Ephesians 6:18; 2 Corinthians 2:10–11)*

Journal Prompt

- What does choosing forgiveness—regardless of your emotions—look like in this situation?

- How might releasing this offense restore the flow of God's grace in your heart and relationships?

Day 21: Warfare in Your Home – Standing for Marriage and Family

Key Scriptures

"For we are not fighting against flesh-and-blood enemies,
but against evil rulers and authorities of the unseen world..."
Ephesians 6:12 (NLT)

"Above all, clothe yourselves with love, which binds us all together in
perfect harmony."
Colossians 3:14 (NLT)

Reflection

Sister, some of the toughest battles happen at home.

Harsh words with your husband. Distant children. Tension thickening the air. These moments leave you discouraged, confused, defeated.

Often, these are spiritual attacks the enemy uses to divide what God wants joined.

The enemy makes you see loved ones as problems—whispering accusations, stirring misunderstandings, pushing reactions over discernment.

Your spouse is not your enemy. Your children are not your enemy. Your home belongs to Jesus.

Clothed in Christ, you stand differently—discerning, not reacting."

Now, clothed in Christ Himself (Days 13–19), you are equipped to face family battles with clarity, authority, and peace. Jesus wore this armor first and won the victory through the cross. Because of Him, you do not fight for victory in your home—you fight from His finished work.

With the Belt of Truth, you reject the lie, *"This marriage is hopeless"*, and stand on God's Word: *"What God has joined together, let no one separate"* (Matthew 19:6). With the Breastplate of Righteousness, you answer a child's outburst not with shame, but with love: *"I love you. I'm here."* With the Shoes of Peace, you pause and say, *"Let's pray together."* With the Shield of Faith, you trust God's promises over today's wandering. And with the Sword of the Spirit, you speak life, blessing, and Scripture over your home.

I have knelt beside empty children's beds, tears falling, praying for their return—not just to me, but to the Lord. The battle was heavy, but even there, God whispered: *I'm working when you cannot see it.*

When I fought spiritual forces instead of people, the atmosphere shifted. Hope returned. Peace grew.

Let His whisper settle: *"Precious, daughter, I am with you in these struggles. I see your longing. You're not alone—I'm working in your home now."*

Your home does not have to remain a battleground.

Because Christ reigns there, it can become a place of healing, peace, and restoration.

Closing Spiritual Seal

You don't strive or control. You trust Jesus' Lordship over what you love most. God works invisibly. Your prayers, love, obedience cultivate peace.

Your home does not have to remain a battleground.

Because Christ reigns there, it can become a place of healing, peace, and restoration.

Application

Before acting, pause and ask the Holy Spirit to show you the deepest need of someone in your home.

Ask yourself: *What would help this person feel most loved or supported today?*

Choose one relationship — your spouse, a child, or another family member — and perform one quiet act of spiritual warfare for them whether it's a prayer, a kind word, or a moment of surrender to God's plan. Trust Him to do the rest:

- Speak a blessing over their pillow before they sleep.

- Write a Scripture and leave it somewhere they will see it.

- Pray aloud over an empty chair, inviting God's peace into that space.

- Play worship music in your home to shift the atmosphere.

- Write a prayer for your family and place it in your Bible as a reminder to intercede daily.

- Anoint the doorframes of your home with oil as a symbol of God's protection and peace.

Then release the outcome to the Lord and trust Him to work in your home.

Prayer

Lord Jesus, Prince of Peace, You have already triumphed over the enemy through the cross. Expose every scheme working against my home.

Forgive me for fighting flesh and blood instead of standing in Your truth. I renounce division, resentment, and fear, trusting that Your resurrection has broken their power.

I ask You to dismantle every spiritual assignment against my marriage, my children, and my household. Clothe our home in Your love and let Your peace rule here.

Fill every room with Your presence.

As for me and my house, we will serve the Lord.

In Your mighty name, Amen.

Take Up Your Sword

(Speak these truths aloud)

- My family is not my enemy. The battle is spiritual. *(Ephesians 6:12)*

- Jesus is Lord over my home, my marriage, and my children. *(Joshua 24:15; Colossians 1:17–18)*

- No weapon formed against my household will prosper. *(Isaiah 54:17)*

- As for me and my house, we will serve the Lord. *(Joshua 24:15)*

Journal Prompt

Where's the enemy creating home division?

What is one way you can respond with Christ's-love today?

End-of-day: How did God work through obedience?

Day 22: Demolishing Strongholds – Freedom in Christ

Key Scripture

We are human, but we don't wage war as humans do. We use God's mighty weapons, not worldly weapons, to knock down the strongholds of human reasoning and to destroy false arguments. We destroy every proud obstacle that keeps people from knowing God. We capture their rebellious thoughts and teach them to obey Christ."
2 Corinthians 10:3-5 (NLT)

Reflection

Sister, picture a stronghold as a locked room deep inside your mind. Its walls are built from old lies — often formed in childhood wounds or traumatic seasons — and the door closes little by little each time you agree with fear, shame, or pain. Before long, that room fills with doubt, anxious thoughts, and false beliefs that shape how you see yourself and God.

A stronghold may look harmless from the outside, but inside it locks away peace and hope, leaving you — or someone you love — trapped. It often begins as a single thought, takes root when we give it permission, and gradually becomes a prison. Fear, addiction, depression, bitterness, and every struggle that feels impossible to escape can begin this way.

For years, even while serving in ministry, I thought strongholds were only obvious things — addictions or destructive habits. If asked, I'd have confidently said no. I didn't realize strongholds begin as *beliefs*, not behaviors.

They are deep thought patterns — shaped by pain, trauma, or repeated lies — that quietly influence how we see God, ourselves, and the world.

Example:

Lie: *"I'm unlovable."*

Truth: *"See how very much our Father loves us, for he calls us his children, and that is what we are!" (1 John 3:1 NLT)*

Strongholds start as beliefs, not behaviors.

Here's the good news: God gave us mighty weapons to demolish strongholds. We don't rely on willpower. We stand on God's Word, Jesus' authority, and the power of the Holy Spirit.

Jesus came to heal the brokenhearted, free captives, open prison doors.

"If the Son sets you free, you will be free indeed." (John 8:36)

Freedom is your inheritance in Christ — unfolding day by day through steady presence and simple disciplines.

Whether a stronghold haunts your mind or loved one's life — addiction, rebellion, depression, fear, family patterns — Jesus won. We stand in victory, speak truth, stop agreeing with lies. Daily practice looks like this: morning truth declarations, quiet moments with God, confessing your need for Him. These choices help your heart and mind embrace the freedom Jesus has already secured for you. I've seen strongholds crumble when people speak God's Word with faith—set free not by effort, but Jesus breaking chains.

The Spirit who raised Jesus lives in you—ready to demolish anything against His truth.

Hear Jesus' whisper now: *"Beloved, I see every battle and lie holding you back. You're not alone—I'm fighting for your freedom. Speak My truth; chains fall. I delight in setting you free."*

Sister, today reclaim enemy territory. Name the stronghold, expose the lie, shatter it with Christ's freedom truth.

Closing Spiritual Seal

Strongholds rarely collapse in a single moment. Think of it like removing bricks from a wall — one lie replaced by truth, one layer at a time.

You are not fighting to become free. You are standing in the freedom Jesus has already won for you. Stay grounded, keep speaking truth, and watch God dismantle what once seemed immovable.

Application

Think of one stronghold you recognize in your life or family — perhaps fear, addiction, bitterness, or hopeless thinking.

Write down the lie behind it. (If you don't know ask the Father to reveal it to you along with His truth).

Then find two or three Scriptures that declare God's truth about that situation. Speak those verses out loud each day. As you continue declaring truth, your faith grows and the stronghold begins to lose its grip.

Prayer

Lord Jesus, You came to set the captives free.

Today I stand in Your authority and use Your mighty weapons to demolish every stronghold in my life and family. I reject every lie and false argument that rises against the knowledge of God.

By Your power, I pull down pride, fear, addiction, and every form of bondage. Set the prisoners free. Let Your truth reign and Your freedom prevail.

In Your mighty, chain-breaking name, Amen.

Take Up Your Sword

(Speak these truths aloud as your offensive weapon today)

- By Your power, Lord, I speak to every stronghold in my life: **Be broken in Jesus' name!** (2 Corinthians 10:3–5)

- Lies and false arguments have no hold on me—God's truth is victorious. (John 8:32; 2 Corinthians 10:5)

- Jesus has set me free, so I am truly free. (John 8:36)

- In Your power, Lord, I proclaim freedom for every captive and the opening of prison doors. (Isaiah 61:1; Luke 4:18

Journal Prompt

What stronghold traps you/someone you love? What Scripture starts demolition today?

Day 23: Weariness & Discouragement – When the Battle Feels Long

Key Scripture

"...He sat down under a solitary broom tree and prayed that he might die. 'I have had enough, LORD,' he said. 'Take my life, for I am no better than my ancestors who have already died.'"
1 Kings 19:4 (NLT)

Reflection

The desert sun pressed down on Elijah's shoulders, the sand hot beneath his feet with every weary step. He could still feel his heart pounding from the chase, the air dry and heavy in his lungs. The lonely cry of a bird echoed in the emptiness, and each breath carried the taste of dust and fatigue. Beneath a solitary broom tree, he sank to the ground, overcome by exhaustion and despair.

Sister, have you ever felt so tired from the struggle that you just wanted to give up? If you've spent years praying for the same thing, facing the same challenges, or carrying the same burden, discouragement can begin to feel like a weight on your soul. If that's where you are today, you are not alone.

Elijah understood that kind of exhaustion. Right after one of the greatest victories in Scripture—when God sent fire on Mount Carmel—Elijah ran in fear, collapsed under a broom tree, and prayed to die. "I have had enough, LORD."

David cried out with the same ache when he asked, "How long, O LORD?" He poured out the anguish of waiting, wondering when God would move and when relief would come.

I have experienced this kind of weariness as well. Battle fatigue. I've mentioned our son's addiction before, but what I haven't shared is that the struggle lasted seventeen long years. There were seasons when hope felt distant, prayers seemed unanswered, and my husband and I were simply worn out. We'd bound everything we knew to bind and loosed everything we knew to loosen. We fasted and prayed. As we watched our son's addiction worsen, we wondered if God had forgotten us or if things would ever change.

Through that long season, we learned that victory doesn't always arrive as a sudden breakthrough. Sometimes it looks like holding on one more day, trusting when you cannot see the way, and praying even when your heart feels empty.

Yet even in the darkest stretches, God would send small reminders of His presence—a kind word from a friend, a Scripture appearing at just the right moment, or an unexpected peace when everything felt impossible. Those small signs became anchors that helped us keep going and reminded us that God was still working, even when the larger answers had not yet come.

Here is the beautiful truth: God meets us in our weariness.

When Elijah collapsed under that broom tree, God did not rebuke him.

Instead, He sent an angel with food and water. Elijah slept, ate, and slept again before God spoke to him.

God restores before He requires.

Notice the order of God's care: nourishment, rest, and strength came before instruction. God's way is compassionate and grace-filled. He does not demand strength from the exhausted—He restores them first.

Jesus extends the same invitation today: come to Him with your weariness, and He will give you rest.

God also promises that when discouragement threatens to overwhelm us, He Himself will strengthen and uphold us. Those words were originally spoken to people living in exile—people who felt forgotten and far from home. Yet the promise still reaches us today: no matter how weary or distant we feel, God remains our strength and help.

Sister, if the battle feels long, turn again to Jesus.

Picture Him offering you a cup of cool water when your spirit feels dry and worn. Let Him nourish your soul, give you rest, and renew your strength.

Listen for His gentle assurance:

"My beloved, I see your weariness and I am near. Let Me carry what has grown too heavy for you. I will uphold you with my strong right arm. You are not alone, and My love for you will never run dry."

Endurance is not defeat.

It is faithfulness in the middle of the fight.

Closing Spiritual Seal

Weariness does not mean you are weak. Often it means you have been faithful for a long time.

God meets you in your exhaustion with grace that sustains you. Staying close to Christ—even when you feel tired—is still forward movement in His kingdom.

Application

Today choose one way to care for your weary soul.

You might take a short nap. Sit quietly and listen to worship music. Repeat Jesus' invitation to rest.

You might also reach out to a trusted friend or prayer partner who can listen and pray with you.

Then bring the hardest battle you are facing before the Lord and ask Him for renewed endurance.

Prayer

Father, I am weary, and the battle has felt long. Thank You for seeing me and meeting me here, just as You met Elijah—with rest before anything else.

Strengthen me when discouragement comes. Hold me up with Your victorious right hand. Renew my hope and help me endure, trusting that You will finish what You have begun.

Today I rest in You.

In your son's name, Amen.

Take Up Your Sword

(Speak these truths aloud)

- Today I hear You say, "Bring Me your weariness, and I will give you rest." (Matthew 11:28)

- Today I hear You say, "You are not forgotten. I strengthen and uphold you." (Isaiah 41:10; Isaiah 49:15–16)

- Today I hear You say, "Discouragement does not define you—I sustain you." (Psalm 55:22; 2 Corinthians 4:8–9)

- Today I hear You say, "Endure in My strength and trust My faithfulness." (Philippians 4:13; Lamentations 3:22–23)

Journal Prompt

What ongoing struggle is wearing you down the most right now?

How do Jesus' invitation to rest and God's promise to strengthen you speak into your weariness today?

Day 24: Fear & Anxiety – Standing When the Threat Feels Constant

Key Scripture

"Don't be afraid, for I am with you. Don't be discouraged, for I am your God. I will strengthen you and help you. I will hold you up with my victorious right hand."
Isaiah 41:10 (NLT)

Reflection

Sister, when discouragement and exhaustion linger, fear, and anxiety often follow. The enemy loves to whisper *"what if "* thoughts that make your heart race and your mind spin. Anxiety itself is not a sin—it's often a signal that something feels out of control. But if it goes unaddressed, it can freeze us in place and steal the peace Jesus intends for us to live in.

God consistently answers fear with His presence. Notice how He repeats His promise: *"Don't be afraid... Don't be discouraged... for I am with you... I am your God."* Our strength does not come from perfect circumstances or from trying to think positively. It comes from knowing that our faithful God is near.

Picture yourself in an ordinary moment—waiting in the carpool line, lying awake at night, or feeling another anxious thought begin to rise. Even there, God whispers, *"I am with you."* His promises are not only for ancient times; they speak into every present moment, reminding you that you are never alone.

Remember, sister, we don't simply wear armor—we are clothed in Christ Himself.

When fear appears, you are already covered by the Prince of Peace.

Remaining close to Him and resting in His presence is your strongest defense against anxiety.

Scripture gives us a practical path forward. Instead of letting worry take over, we bring our concerns to God in prayer, telling Him what we need and thanking Him for what He has already done. When we do this, His peace guards our hearts and minds as we live in Christ.

One simple way to practice this is by thanking God for something specific each time you pray. You might say, *"Thank You for the friend who texted me yesterday,"* or *"Thank You for the sunrise this morning."* Naming real gifts—even small ones—anchors your heart in gratitude and helps open the door to God's peace.

Peace grows through trust. Sometimes it arrives in a moment; other times it develops slowly over days or weeks. As we keep turning our attention back to God instead of the problem, His peace begins to settle in. If calm does not come instantly, that does not mean you're failing—it simply means you are learning to trust Him step by step.

I have walked through seasons when anxiety felt relentless. There were nights when fear tightened my chest and days when *"what if"* thoughts repeated in my mind. When the phone rang in the middle of the night, my heart pounded with the fear every parent dreads—*Was this the call? Had our son overdosed or one of our daughters been in an accident?*

At times it felt unbearable.

But when I began turning those worries into prayers— *"Lord, I don't know what to do, but my eyes are on You"*—His peace came. Sometimes it came slowly, but it always came. When my strength was gone, He carried me.

Sister, the threat may feel constant, but God's presence is even more steady. Stay close to your Prince of Peace. Turn your worries into prayers. Fix your thoughts on Him and allow His peace to guard your heart and mind.

And remember, if anxiety ever becomes overwhelming or too heavy to carry alone, there is wisdom in seeking support from a trusted counselor or professional. God often brings help through wise and caring people. Reaching out is an act of courage, not weakness.

Closing Spiritual Seal

Fear may come near, but it does not get the final word—God's presence does.

Feeling anxious does not mean you lack faith; it simply means you are human in an uncertain world.

As you remain close to Christ, His peace steadies your heart and reminds you that you are securely held by the One who never lets go.

Application

Today, if fear or anxiety rises, pause and pray the promise of peace aloud.

Tell God exactly what you are worried about, thank Him for what He has already done, and ask Him to fill your heart with His peace.

Each time the worry returns, repeat this practice. Over time, prayer begins to replace panic.

Prayer

Father, I bring my fear and anxiety to You today. Thank You for being with me and for being my God. I choose to pray instead of worry.

Here are my burdens. Please give me Your peace that goes beyond understanding. Guard my heart and mind in Christ Jesus. Help me keep my thoughts focused on You and hold me up with Your strong right hand.

In Jesus' name, Amen.

Right now, pause for sixty seconds of quiet. Close your eyes and rest in the truth that you are held by God. Let your breathing slow, notice His nearness, and receive His peace.

Take Up Your Sword

(Speak these truths aloud)

- I will not be afraid or discouraged—God is with me. (Joshua 1:9; Isaiah 41:10)

- I will not worry. I will talk to God about everything and receive His peace. (Philippians 4:6–7)

- I fix my mind on God, and He fills me with perfect peace. (Isaiah 26:3)

- God strengthens and upholds me. Fear and anxiety do not control my life. (Isaiah 41:10; 2 Timothy 1:7)

Journal Prompt

What fear or anxiety feels most constant in your life right now?

How does turning that fear into prayer and focusing on God's presence begin to change your response today?

Day 25: Depression & Heaviness — When Darkness Presses In

Key Scripture

"Why am I discouraged? Why is my heart so sad? I will put my hope in God! I will praise him again — my Savior and my God."
Psalm 42:5 (NLT)

Reflection

Sister, if darkness surrounds you and heaviness weighs you down, you are not alone. Feeling this way does not mean you are failing God. Depression and heaviness can appear through grief, trauma, exhaustion, or chemical and hormonal changes that make everything feel heavier.

The enemy uses these moments to whisper lies: *"This will never lift," "God is far away,"* or *"You're too broken to be used."*

Pause now, sister. What lie has the enemy fed you this week? Write it down.

Naming it weakens its power and begins telling truth with God. Don't stop there, ask the Lord to speak truth in its place, and write what He brings to mind.

Your feelings do not separate you from God's love or presence. Jesus was *"a man of sorrows, acquainted with deepest grief."* Picture Him in Gethsemane — tears on His face, sweating drops of blood in his anguish, praying in darkness while carrying the world's weight. **He understands overwhelming sorrow.**

Lament is not weak faith — it is faith that keeps speaking in the dark.

The Psalms hold honest prayers from David, Asaph, and the sons of Korah. In Psalm 42, the writer questions his downcast soul but turns back to hope: *"I will put my hope in God! I will praise him again—my Savior and my God."*

I have walked roads of time when joy felt distant and every day carried heavy emotional, spiritual, and physical weight. I brought real sadness to Jesus as it was. Healing came slowly through prayer, Scripture, worship, and support from others. One season required wise medical care alongside spiritual help—talking with a Christian counselor and my family doctor. Those steps showed faith, not lack of it.

God brings healing through both.

Sister, if darkness presses in, you do not need to force feeling better now. Bring heaviness to Jesus, the Man of Sorrows who carries your pain. If praise feels impossible, pause thirty seconds, breathe slowly, and whisper: *"Jesus, I put my hope in You."*

Even a breath prayer is faith when words fail. He draws especially close to the brokenhearted.

Closing Spiritual Seal

Heaviness does not disqualify you; it reveals your need for God's sustaining grace.

Even in the darkness, His presence surrounds you and gently holds you steady.

As you remain in Christ, light will return in His time and in His way.

Application

Today choose one psalm of lament—perhaps Psalm 13, Psalm 42, or Psalm 88—and let it walk with you through the day.

Hold onto one phrase that speaks to your heart. Repeat it slowly when heaviness returns.

Add a simple declaration of trust: *"Yet I will hope in You."*

If the heaviness continues, consider reaching out to a trusted friend, pastor, counselor, or medical professional. God often sends help through the people He places around us.

Prayer

Lord Jesus, Man of Sorrows, You understand the heaviness I carry.

Today I bring my sadness, exhaustion, and darkness to You without shame.

Meet me here. Lift the weight I cannot carry on my own.

Renew my hope—even if it begins as something very small today.

Surround me with Your presence and send the help I need, whether spiritual, emotional, or physical.

I choose to put my hope in You again. Be my light in this valley.

In your precious name, I pray, Amen.

Take Up Your Sword

(Speak these truths aloud. As you do, consider standing, opening your hands, or placing a hand over your heart as a physical reminder of trust.)

- You are close to the brokenhearted; You rescue crushed spirits." (Psalm 34:18)

- I put my hope in God; I will praise Him again—my Savior and my God. (Psalm 42:5)

- The Lord sustains me; I will not remain downcast forever. (Psalm 55:22; Psalm 30:5)

- Weeping may last for the night, but joy comes morning." (Psalm 30:5)

Journal Prompt

What lie feeds your heaviness most?

What truth does Psalm 42:5 speak into your darkness today?

Day 26: Hope That Holds – Steady Confidence in Christ

Key Scripture

*"This hope is a strong and trustworthy anchor for our souls.
It leads us through the curtain into God's inner sanctuary."*
Hebrews 6:19 (NLT)

Reflection

Sister, can you feel the weight of darkness pressing in, the kind that settles heavy on your chest before your feet even touch the floor? Maybe you wake up and the world still feels gray, the coffee warm in your hands but your heart aching for light. The breakthrough has not come, the pain is still real, and tomorrow looks much like today. You are still standing, but it feels like you are standing in the middle of a storm with wind whipping around you and hope seeming just out of reach.

The enemy tries to steal our hope in those quiet moments when the house is still and your soul aches. He whispers that you are alone and that nothing will change. God hasn't answered because he's not going to. Depression and discouragement often attack hope because the enemy knows how closely hope and faith are connected. Scripture tells us that faith is the reality of what we hope for, the evidence of what we cannot yet see. Without hope, faith has nothing to hold onto.

Biblical hope is not the same as simple optimism. As Pastor William Sloane Coffin once said, *"Hope is a state of mind independent of the state of the world. If your heart is full of hope, you can be persistent even when you cannot be optimistic."*

Biblical hope is deeper than positive thinking. It does not pretend everything is fine when it is not. It does not deny pain or demand that we just believe harder. Instead, it is a steady, Christ-centered confidence that God remains faithful even when we cannot yet see how.

Hope is a strong and trustworthy anchor for our souls,
leading us into God's presence.

Hebrews calls this hope "a strong and trustworthy anchor for our souls." **An anchor does not remove the storm; it keeps the ship from drifting.** Other Scriptures echo the same truth. Hope does not disappoint because God pours His love into our hearts through the Holy Spirit. Through the resurrection of Jesus Christ, we have a living hope that no grave can silence. Even suffering can deepen hope. Trials produce perseverance, perseverance shapes character, and character strengthens hope. Hope often grows strongest in the very places we feared it might die.

Hope feels like light slowly breaking through heavy clouds. It rarely arrives as a sudden sunrise. More often it begins as a quiet glow that grows until you realize you can see the path forward again.

I know what it is to have hope feel fragile. Darkness lingered, prayers seemed unanswered, and I wondered if I would ever feel steady again. In those moments, I held on to Jesus, my Living Hope. The deeper truth is that He was holding on to me. In the waiting, this quiet hope began to take root. It was not dramatic or loud. It was simply Jesus, my Anchor, holding me steady when I could not hold on myself. He never let go.

Imagine Him whispering gently to your heart right now: *"Beloved, I am with you in the waiting. Let My presence comfort you. Lean into Me, for I am closer than your next breath. Trust that I am working in ways you cannot yet see."*

Sister, if you are tired of waiting for the clouds to part, lean into this hope today. It does not rush you. It does not shame you.

It simply holds you steady in the One who rose from the dead.

Closing Spiritual Seal

Even when your grip feels weak, Christ's hold on you is strong.

You are not drifting, and you are not forgotten.

This quiet hope is already anchoring your soul.

Application

Today choose one Scripture that speaks hope over your situation. Read it slowly and speak it aloud.

Reflect on what that promise means for the battle you are facing. Carry that verse with you throughout the day, repeating it whenever discouragement rises.

Let its truth become the anchor that steadies your heart.

Prayer

Lord Jesus, my Anchor and my Living Hope, thank You for a hope that never disappoints.

When darkness lingers and weariness presses in, hold me steady. Grow resilient hope within me through every trial. Let Your love fill my heart again and remind me that You are faithful.

Even when I cannot see the way forward, I trust that You are leading me. In Your precious name, Amen

Take Up Your Sword

(Speak these truths aloud)

- This hope is my strong anchor; my soul is secure in Christ. (Hebrews 6:19)

- God's hope does not disappoint; His love fills my heart. (Romans 5:5)

- I have a living hope through the resurrection of Jesus. (1 Peter 1:3)

- As I wait on the Lord, my strength and hope grow stronger. (Romans 5:3–4; Isaiah 40:31)

Journal Prompt

What does steady, resilient hope look like in your current battle?

How has Jesus been your anchor in past seasons of waiting, and how might that memory strengthen your hope today?

Day 27: Prodigals – Standing in Faith for Those You Love

Key Scripture

"So he returned home to his father. And while he was still a long way off, his father saw him coming. Filled with love and compassion, he ran to his son, embraced him, and kissed him."
Luke 15:20 (NLT)

Reflection

Sister, if you are praying for a prodigal—a child who has wandered, a spouse who feels distant, or a loved one struggling with addiction, rebellion, or unbelief—you know how painful it is to stand between God's promise and the reality you see.

It can feel like standing barefoot in the cold dawn, the ache of waiting settling deep in your chest, your prayers rising in the stillness like breath in winter air. We spoke about hope yesterday because this journey can often feel hopeless. I know it did for me.

There were seasons when the more I prayed, the worse things seemed to become. Some mornings felt like walking through thick fog—each step forward swallowed by disappointment, hope slipping through my fingers like water. My endurance and faith were tested in ways I never expected.

Waiting for a prodigal stretches your heart in ways few other battles do.

But here is what God taught me during those long years: we can hold onto hope without trying to control everything, and we can have faith without pretending the pain is not real. We do not have to force results or try to manage the outcome for God.

Instead, we stand in the gap — trusting His heart even when we cannot see His work.

In Jesus' parable of the prodigal son, the father did not chase his son into the distant country or force him to return. He waited. He watched. And when the son finally turned toward home, the father ran to meet him.

Our heavenly Father is even more loving and attentive than the father in that story. He sees our prodigals long before we do, and He is already working in ways we cannot see. Scripture promises that God Himself fights for our children and rescues them *(Isaiah 49:25)*.

I lived through this battle while praying over my daughters and during the many long years, while my son struggled with addiction. There were nights when I cried out, "Lord, how much longer?" The waiting felt endless.

But in that season God taught me to stand — not by fixing the situation, but by trusting Him when everything looked worse. I learned to pray bold promises over my son, to speak hope even when the facts looked hopeless, and to release control again and again and again into God's hands.

When the breakthrough finally came, it was not because I fixed anything.

The Father waits, watches, runs to meet.

It was because the Father ran when my prodigal turned.

Even in the long, quiet hours of waiting, **listen for the gentle whisper of Jesus:**

"Beloved, I see every tear you have cried in the dark. I am holding you just as surely as I am holding the one you are praying for. I am working in the waiting, weaving hope into every moment—even when you cannot see it yet."

Sister, your prodigal is not too far gone.
Keep standing.
Keep praying.
Keep loving without trying to control.
Your faith is not wasted. God is fighting for them.

Closing Spiritual Seal

Waiting does not mean nothing is happening. God is working in ways you cannot see. Even when your heart feels tired, the Father has not turned away.

You are not carrying this burden alone. He is watching, waiting, and ready to run—to you and to the one you love.

Application

Choose one promise from Scripture to pray over your prodigal today.

Write their name beside the verse and place it somewhere you will see it often. Speak that promise aloud each day as an act of faith while you wait.

Prayer

Father, You see my prodigal, and You love them more than I ever could.

Today I release control and stand in faith between Your promise and this pain. Fight for them. Draw them home. Break every chain that binds them.

Give me endurance to keep praying and hope that does not waver. Thank You that Jesus Himself is interceding for us even now.

I trust that You are already moving toward my prodigal with mercy and love.

In the mighty name of Jesus, Amen.

Take Up Your Sword

(Speak these truths aloud)

- I stand in faith for my prodigal. God fights for them and rescues my children. (Isaiah 49:25)

- The Father watches and waits. He runs to meet the one who turns toward home. (Luke 15:20)

- No one is too far gone. The blood of Jesus reaches even the farthest wanderer. (Isaiah 1:18; Romans 5:8)

- My prayers matter. God is working in His perfect time. (1 John 5:14–15; James 5:16)

Journal Prompt

What promise are you holding onto for your prodigal today?

How does releasing control and trusting God's heart—even when circumstances look worse—change the way you pray and hope?

Promises to Pray Over a Prodigal

Sister, God honors free will—He woos hearts without forcing, even when our mother-love aches for breakthrough. Here are **8 Scripture-based prayer strategies** that balance their choice with His relentless pursuit.

1 – Heart-Softening Prayer

"Father, soften their heart with Your kindness that leads to repentance (Romans 2:4).
Stir hunger for home like the prodigal in his pigpen (Luke 15:17)."

Focus: Holy Spirit conviction without coercion.

2 – Wooing Prayer

"Lord, draw them with lovingkindness—the everlasting love that never quits (Jeremiah 31:3).
Use cords of human kindness, not force (Hosea 11:4)."

Focus: God's gentle pursuit respects choice.

3 – Eyes-to-See Prayer

*"Open their eyes to Your goodness in their land (Psalm 34:8).
Let them taste and see You're better than sin's empty promises (Isaiah
55:6-7)."*

Focus: Revelation breaks deception.

4 – Homesick Prayer

*"Awaken prodigal homesickness. Make the far country bitter,
Your welcome sweet (Luke 15:17-18).
Turn their feet toward home."*

Focus: Their will bends homeward.

5 – Patience Prayer

*"Thank You for patience—not wanting any to perish, but all to reach repentance (2
Peter 3:9). Your timing perfect, their response sovereign."*

Focus: God's long-suffering grace.

6 – Surrender Prayer

*"Holy Spirit, convict of sin, righteousness, judgment (John 16:8-11).
Let surrender feel like freedom, not chains."*

Focus: Truth liberates their choice.

7 – Father-Running Prayer

*"Position them to turn—one step homeward—and You run
with compassion (Luke 15:20).
Ready the robe, ring, feast."*

Focus: Celebrate their decision point.

8 – Awakening Prayer

*"Father, bring them to themselves like the prodigal in the
pigpen—'coming to his senses' amid hunger and ruin (Luke 15:17).
For addicts, lead to safe addiction's end, restored sanity through
Your discipline (Hebrews 12:11).
Awaken realization: Father's house abundant, sin's way empty."*

Focus: Self-realization + safe recovery turning point

Remember sister, "Nothing is impossible with God." (Luke 1:37)

Write one of these verses where you can see it often and pray it daily over the person you love. I pray, He strengthens you in the waiting and uplifts you when you are disheartened.

Day 28: Perseverance – Fighting the Long War Well

Key Scripture

"So, let's not get tired of doing what is good. At just the right time we will reap a harvest of blessing if we do not give up."
Galatians 6:9 (NLT)

Reflection

Feel the burn in your legs as you push through one more mile. Gravel crunches beneath your feet, sweat stings your eyes, and your heartbeat pounds in your chest. The air feels thick, each breath reminding you how far you have come — and how far you still have to go. The finish line is hidden, the journey relentless, yet you keep moving forward. Every step becomes a quiet act of courage.

Perseverance yields a harvest if you do not give up.

Sister, some battles feel like sprints, but most resemble marathons. The enemy's strategy in a long struggle is simple: wear you down.

He whispers, *"How much longer?"*
He presses, *"Nothing is changing."*

He tempts you to stop praying, stop believing, and stop standing — often right before the breakthrough.

But God calls us to perseverance, a steady endurance that refuses to quit. It is not loud or dramatic. It is the quiet, daily choice to keep walking in obedience, trusting His strength rather than your own.

Galatians reminds us not to grow weary in doing good, because a harvest will come at the right time if we do not give up.

Hebrews encourages us to run the race set before us with endurance, fixing our eyes on Jesus — the One who began our faith and will bring it to completion. When we remember all that He endured, we find strength to keep going.

Jesus did not quit.

He endured the cross for the joy set before Him.

And now He runs the race beside us.

Running is something my family understands well. My daughter Tiffany and my son Brandon — yes, the same son I prayed for during seventeen long years of addiction — are both runners. Recently he completed a 65-mile ultramarathon, while I ran 30 miles.

We know the difference between a sprint and a long race.

A sprint is powered by adrenaline.

A long run requires pacing, endurance, and determination when your body aches and your mind begs you to stop.

Victory does not happen at mile one. It comes when you cross the finish line after hours of steady effort — and months of training before the race ever began.

Faithfulness is not measured by where you are in the race. It is
measured by your willingness to keep running.

That is how it was with our prayers.

There were seasons when hope felt thin and the road seemed endless. But we kept moving forward—praying, believing, and persevering.

When my son finally crossed his own finish line into freedom, we saw the harvest. It did not come because the race was short. It came because we did not stop running.

And neither should you.

Imagine Jesus speaking encouragement to your weary heart:

"Daughter, I see your struggle, and I am right beside you. I will never leave you. Lean on Me. Every step you take brings you closer to the joy I have promised."

Sister, if your struggle feels long, it does not mean you're failing. It means you're persevering.
Keep doing good.
Keep praying. Keep standing.
The harvest is coming—at exactly the right time.

Closing Spiritual Seal

Jesus once said that the one who endures to the end will be saved.

God is preparing a harvest that will arrive at the appointed time—not a moment early and not a moment late.

Stay in the race.

Grace will carry you to the finish line.

Application

Identify one area where you feel tempted to give up.

Speak the promise of perseverance aloud over that situation. Then take one small step of obedience today—pray again, send that encouraging message, or choose faith in a moment where you once felt discouraged.

Perseverance often grows through small acts of faithfulness.

Prayer

Lord Jesus, Champion of my faith, thank You for enduring the cross for me.

When I grow weary and feel tempted to quit, help me fix my eyes on You. Strengthen me so I do not grow tired of doing what is good. Root my heart in Your faithfulness and help me persevere until the harvest comes.

Hold me steady until the finish line. In your precious name I pray, Amen.

Take Up Your Sword

(Speak these truths aloud)

- I will not grow weary in doing good; I will reap a harvest if I don't give up. (Galatians 6:9)

- I run with endurance, fixing my eyes on Jesus who endured for me. (Hebrews 12:1–3)

- God is faithful. He strengthens me in the long battle. (2 Thessalonians 3:3; 1 Corinthians 1:9)

- Perseverance leads to victory. I will not quit. (Matthew 24:13; James 1:12)

Journal Prompt

Where is the enemy trying to wear you down right now?

How does fixing your eyes on Jesus—and remembering past harvests God has brought in your life—strengthen you to keep going today?

Day 29: Victory That Lasts – Building a Life of Resistance

Key Scripture

"So humble yourselves before God. Resist the devil, and he will flee from you. Come close to God, and God will come close to you."
James 4:7–8 (NLT)

Reflection

Every victory over temptation begins by drawing close to Jesus, who equips us to resist the enemy's schemes. Just as a runner builds endurance mile by mile, or a weightlifter grows stronger with each repetition, every moment you spend with Jesus increases your spiritual stamina and resistance against the enemy.

Resistance flows from relationship, not striving.

Sister, victory in spiritual warfare is not a single event—it is a way of life. The enemy never takes a break and constantly searches for opportunities to gain ground. Lasting victory does not come from emotional highs or dramatic moments. It grows through daily habits that keep you close to Jesus, grounded in His presence, and connected to His people.

James gives us a simple pattern for victory: *"Humble yourselves before God. Resist the devil, and he will flee from you. Come close to God, and God will come close to you."*

Notice the order. Humility. Closeness. Resistance.

We humble ourselves. We come close to God first. Resistance flows from relationship, not from trying harder. When you stay near Him—clothed in Christ as your armor—the enemy has less space to work.

Picture the quiet hush of early morning, when you whisper His name and sense His presence wrapping around you like a warm shawl. The enemy prowls at the edges, hoping you will wander off alone. But the Lord invites you into the circle of His people, where encouragement rings like laughter around a dinner table.

Daily practices matter:

- Begin your day by putting on Christ and praying the armor prayer.

- Stay in Scripture, letting God's Word renew your mind.

- Pray throughout the day—short breath prayers, honest conversations with God, and moments of thanksgiving.

- Worship, even when it feels difficult, because praise strengthens your spirit.

I have seen how powerful this can be in my own family. My daughter Destiny is a gifted worship leader, but during a difficult season in ministry—after the heartbreak of two miscarriages—she struggled to engage in worship.

The pain felt heavier than her ability to sing. During one service, as the song *"I Live to Worship You"* was being sung, she stood there frustrated and ashamed that her grief felt stronger than her worship. In that moment, she sensed the Lord whisper to her heart: *"You have an 'Oh' though. Just give Me the 'Oh.'"*

With tears streaming down her face, she lifted her voice and joined the chorus: *"When you've done all you can do and said all you can say, cry out. Ooh-oh, oh-oh. Ooh-oh, oh-oh."*

Sometimes worship begins with nothing more than a cry. Even that simple offering draws us back into God's presence. Sister, give Him you 'Oh'.

Community is also essential. Scripture reminds us that two people together are stronger than one. As Ecclesiastes teaches, *"Two people are better off than one, for they can help each other succeed... A cord of three strands is not easily broken"* (Ecclesiastes 4:9–12). When believers stand together in prayer and truth, their strength multiplies. Isolation is where the enemy works most easily; community is God's design for lasting victory.

Finally, establish wise guardrails—loving boundaries that protect your heart and home. Limit what feeds fear or comparison. Say no to habits or relationships that steal your peace. Watch over your thoughts, your words, and how you spend your time. These are not restrictions; they are ways to protect the freedom Christ has already given you.

Imagine Jesus speaking this invitation to your heart: *"Beloved, rest in My presence and let Me be your strength. When you abide in Me, you are never fighting alone. Walk with Me daily, and My peace will guard your heart and mind."*

Sister, you are already clothed in Christ. Now build a life that resists the enemy—not by striving harder, but by staying close to Jesus.

Closing Spiritual Seal

Lasting victory grows from staying near to Christ. When you remain clothed in Him, rooted in truth, and connected to His people, the enemy loses his footing.

This victory is steady, practiced, and sustained by grace—and it is already taking root in your life.

Application

Choose one spiritual habit to strengthen this week—perhaps morning prayer, daily Scripture reading, or reaching out to a trusted sister in faith.

Then set one small guardrail to protect your peace. This might mean limiting social media, adjusting your evening routine, or saying no to something that drains you.

Focus on consistency rather than intensity.

Consider reaching out to a trusted friend today and inviting her to walk this journey with you.

Prayer

Lord Jesus, today I draw close to You.

Thank You for promising that when I come near to You, You draw near to me. Help me build habits that keep me abiding in Your presence—through prayer, Your Word, worship, and community.

Give me wisdom to set healthy guardrails that protect the victory You have already won for me. Let my life reflect steady resistance to the enemy and deep peace in You.

I your name, I pray, Amen.

Take Up Your Sword

(Speak these truths aloud)

- I draw close to God, and He draws close to me. The enemy must flee. (James 4:7–8; Psalm 145:18)

- I abide in Christ daily; His presence is my victory. (John 15:4–5; 1 Corinthians 15:57)

- I am stronger in community; my strength multiplies as I stand with others. (Ecclesiastes 4:9–12; Deuteronomy 32:30)

- I build wise guardrails and live in the freedom Christ gives. (Galatians 5:1; Proverbs 4:23)

Journal Prompt

What daily practice or guardrail could you strengthen this week to make victory sustainable?

How has staying close to Jesus protected you in past battles?

Day 30: Armed & Victorious – Standing Firm in Christ

Key Scripture

"Be strong in the Lord and in His mighty power. Put on all of God's armor so that you will be able to stand firm against all the strategies of the devil."
Ephesians 6:10–11 (NLT)

Reflection

The day has finally arrived.

Imagine the gentle hush of anticipation settling over the room as the soft glow of candlelight flickers across faces eager and expectant. The scent of anointing oil mingles with the faint aroma of fresh flowers, symbolizing new beginnings and sacred purpose. You feel the warmth of hands pressed upon your shoulders, their touch both steadying and empowering, as prayers of blessing fill the air.

A resounding chorus of voices rises in worship, echoing off the walls—each note a reminder that you do not stand alone. The weight of the mantle—both literal and spiritual—rests upon you, pressing in with holy significance and the promise of God's presence. Tears shimmer in eyes and run down cheeks, mingling joy and reverence as hearts respond to the call.

The sound of Scripture being spoken over you rings clear and true, every word a declaration of your identity and authority in Christ. As you take your first step forward, the floor beneath you feels solid—firm with the assurance that Christ goes before you and walks beside you.

Sister, today is your commissioning day.

You have spent these past thirty days awakening to the reality of the battle, learning to clothe yourself in Christ, and practicing how to stand firm through seasons of weariness, fear, waiting, and perseverance. You have discovered that spiritual warfare is not about striving harder—it is about abiding deeper.

The victory you seek has never rested on your strength. It rests on Jesus.
From the beginning, God never intended for you to fight alone. Scripture tells us to *"be strong in the Lord and in His mighty power."* The strength you need for every battle flows from Him.

When you put on the armor of God, you are not simply putting on spiritual tools. You are putting on Christ Himself—His truth, His righteousness, His peace, His faithfulness, His salvation, and His living Word.

This is what it means to be **armed and victorious**.

Victory does not mean the battle disappears. It means you stand in the finished work of Christ while the battle continues around you.

There will still be days when the fight feels long. There will still be moments when the enemy whispers lies or tries to stir fear, discouragement, or weariness. But now you know where to stand.

You stand in Christ.
You stand clothed in His armor. You stand rooted in His truth.
The enemy may still attempt to attack, but he cannot take ground where Christ already reigns.

Think back over these past days. You have learned to awaken to the battle, stand strong in God's power, clothe yourself in Christ, guard your heart against offense, demolish lies, persevere through long seasons, and build habits that keep you close to Jesus.

This is not the end of the journey.
It is the beginning of a new way of living. A life of steady resistance.
A life of abiding.
A life where victory is not a moment, but a daily walk with Christ.

Imagine Jesus speaking these words to your heart today:

"Beloved, the battle is real, but you are not alone in this battle. I have already overcome the world. Walk with Me, remain in Me, and My victory will be your strength. Stand firm, and do not be afraid."

Sister, you are clothed in Christ. You are equipped with His armor.

You are surrounded by His presence. You are **armed and victorious**.

Stand firm.

Closing Spiritual Seal

The battle may continue, but the outcome has already been decided. Jesus has overcome the world, and you stand in His victory.

Walk forward with confidence, clothed in Christ, strengthened by His Spirit, and anchored in His truth.

You are not merely surviving the battle. You are standing victorious in Him.

Application

Today, take a few minutes to reflect on what God has taught you over these thirty days.

Write down one truth you want to carry forward and one habit you want to continue practicing.

Then pray and dedicate this next season of your life to walking daily in Christ's strength.

Prayer

Lord Jesus, thank You for walking with me through these thirty days.

Thank You for teaching me to stand strong in You. Help me continue putting on Your armor each day and living close to Your heart.

Strengthen me for every battle ahead. Keep me rooted in Your truth, filled with Your peace, and steady in Your presence.

I choose to walk forward in Your victory. In Your mighty name, Amen.

Take Up Your Sword

(Speak these truths aloud)

- I am strong in the Lord and in His mighty power. (Ephesians 6:10)

- I put on the full armor of God and stand firm. (Ephesians 6:11)

- In Christ I have victory over every scheme of the enemy. (Romans 8:37; 1 Corinthians 15:57)

- Greater is He who is in me than he who is in the world. (1 John 4:4)

Journal Prompt

Looking back over these thirty days, what truth about spiritual victory has changed your perspective the most?

What daily practice will help you continue standing strong in Christ from this day forward?

A Final Note from the Author

Sister, you did it.
You are armed.
You are victorious.
Now go—and watch Him do greater things through you.
May I have the honor of praying over you?

Father, in the mighty name of Your Son, Jesus,

I pray that You would be with my sister as she goes forth in the power of Your strength.

She is clothed in Your righteousness, walking in Your peace, girded with Your truth, and protected from every fiery dart by the shield of faith. Her mind is covered with the helmet of salvation, and her hand grips and wields the sword of the Spirit—Your living Word.

She is more than a conqueror. She fights from a place of victory. She is an overcomer by the blood of the Lamb and the word of her testimony.

Help her remain close to You each day—abiding in Your presence, rooted in Your Word, and strengthened by Your Spirit.

Shelter her beneath Your wings. Uphold her with Your strong right hand and guide her with Your eye.

Guard her heart from fear, offense, discouragement, and weariness. Fill her with faith, peace, and courage.

May she always know You—and know who she is in You.

She is Your beloved daughter, an heir with Jesus to the Kingdom.
Chosen.
Redeemed.
Loved.
Commissioned.
Amen.

With all my love and faith,

Lesa Henderson

Continue the Journey

Sister, the end of these thirty days is not the end of the journey. Spiritual victory is not a single moment—it is a life lived close to Jesus. The battles may continue, but you now know where to stand; in Christ.

Keep putting on the armor each day. Stay rooted in God's Word. Remain connected to believers who will pray with you and encourage your faith. Continue bringing every battle to the Lord, remembering that the victory was already secured through Jesus.

If this devotional encouraged you, consider walking through it again in a future season. Each time you return, the Holy Spirit may highlight new truths and strengthen different areas of your life.

You might also consider inviting a small group of women—friends, a Bible study group, or women from your church—to go through these thirty days together. Praying, sharing, and standing in faith together strengthens the body of Christ and multiplies the impact of what God is doing.

Wherever the Lord leads you next, remember this truth: You are clothed in Christ.

You are strengthened by His Spirit. You are standing in His victory.

Walk forward with confidence.

Stay Connected

If this devotional blessed you, I would love to stay connected with you.

You can find additional devotionals, encouragement, and updates about future books and resources here:

Website: https://www.lesahenderson.com/
Email: lesa@lesahenderson.com

Social Media:

https://www.pinterest.com/lesahenderson
https://www.instagram.com/lesahenderson
https://x.com/LesaHenderson
https://www.facebook.com/WWarriorsofGod

If *Armed & Victorious* encouraged you, consider sharing it with a friend or leaving a review where you purchased the book. Your review helps other women discover the message of victory in Christ.

Thank you for allowing me to walk with you on this journey.

About the Author

Lesa Henderson is an author, filmmaker, and minister with a passion for helping women walk in the freedom, authority, and victory that belong to them in Christ.

Through writing, teaching, and storytelling, Lesa encourages believers to move beyond fear-based spiritual warfare and instead live from the place of intimacy, identity, and abiding in Jesus. Her work focuses on helping women recognize the enemy's schemes, stand firm in God's truth, and experience the peace and strength that come from a life rooted in Christ.

Lesa is also the author of Laurel Ridge Books, inspirational & inspirational suspense fiction that weaves faith, redemption, and courage into compelling stories. Her creative background in storytelling and film allows her to bring vivid imagery and real-life testimony into her devotional writing, making biblical truth both practical and deeply personal.

Her heart is to see women strengthened in their faith, restored in hope, and equipped to walk confidently in the victory Jesus has already won.

Lesa lives with her husband, Ken in Florida where they pastor Salt Life Church and continues to write, speak, and create stories that inspire faith and perseverance.

A Final Blessing

May the Lord bless you and keep you.
May His presence go before you and remain with you in every battle.
May you walk each day clothed in Christ, strengthened by His Spirit, and anchored in His Word.
Stand firm.
Remain close to Jesus.
And remember—you are **armed and victorious**.

Discussion Guide for Individuals or Small Groups

This devotional can be experienced alone or with a small group of women who desire to grow stronger in Christ and stand firm in spiritual victory. These questions are designed to help you reflect more deeply on the themes of each section and encourage meaningful conversation.

You may wish to read several devotions together each week and then use the questions below to guide your discussion and prayer time.

Section I: Awakening to the Battle

1. Before reading this section, how did you understand spiritual warfare? Did anything challenge or reshape your perspective?

2. Why do you think the enemy often targets our identity in Christ first?

3. Which truth about who you are in Christ impacted you the most?

4. How does understanding that Christ has already won the victory change the way you approach spiritual battles?

5. Which declaration from the *Take Up Your Sword* sections strengthened your faith the most?

Close your discussion by praying for one another to walk confidently in your identity in Christ.

Section II: Clothed in Christ

1. Which piece of the armor of God felt most meaningful or personally relevant to you?

2. How can you intentionally "put on Christ" in your daily life?

3. Which devotion in this section spoke most directly to your current circumstances?

4. What habits help you remain rooted in God's Word and truth when the enemy tries to bring discouragement or lies?

5. How can speaking Scripture aloud strengthen your spiritual resistance?

Take time to pray together, asking the Lord to help each of you remain clothed in Christ daily.

Section III: Advancing with Steadfastness

1. Which devotion in this section encouraged you during a season of weariness, waiting, or spiritual struggle?

2. Why is forgiveness important in protecting our hearts during spiritual battles?

3. How does hope anchor us when circumstances seem unchanged?

4. What practical habits will help you remain close to Jesus after completing this devotional?

5. Looking back over the entire journey, what truth has impacted you most?

Close your time by praying that each woman would continue walking in Christ's victory and strength.

www.ingramcontent.com/pod-product-compliance
Lightning Source LLC
Chambersburg PA
CBHW051441130726
47987CB00005B/2137